THE *Just Delicious* COOK BOOK

The
Just Delicious Cook Book
created for sophisticated palates and
robust appetites. Illustrated and
written by Ruth Mellinkoff

The Ward Ritchie Press · Los Angeles

Contents

Introduction

Just Delicious IS THE THIRD episode of my continued interest in how to prepare exciting and delectable food without soul-searing manipulations in the kitchen and without last minute hair-raising chaos before guests arrive. Gustatory experiences abroad have provided a base for many of my recipes in this cook book. I first noted the more memorable moments at table in a journal I usually keep while traveling; at home I then used my notes and collected impressions as a point of departure for creating dishes that reflect rather than duplicate foods and feasts I enjoyed abroad. The delectations from abroad therefore are not carbon copy replicas; they are free and sometimes wild interpretations of my own. On rare and brief occasions we lived in London and Paris where I was able to cook *in situ;* a few of those preparations are also included and can be easily identified by place names such as Avenue Wagram and Sloane Square in the recipe titles.

Travel was not the only source of inspiration for the delectations in *Just Delicious.* Ideas for other recipes came from every imaginable place and in wondrous ways: photographs of beautifully prepared food; conscious attempts to produce some of my daydreaming gastronomic fantasies; and contributions from friends with marvelous palates and unusual culinary skills. Other recipes evolved from numerous collages constructed from whatever ingredients I might have on hand in the kitchen at any particular moment. Serendipity provided the rest.

But whatever the genesis of the recipes, the emphasis in this book —as in my *Something Special Cook Book* and *The Uncommon Cook Book*—is on beforehand preparation. Each recipe therefore includes information about: 1.) preparation ahead of time, and 2.) freezing (if appropriate). The recipes have been grouped together under simple chapter headings that may not be descriptive of all their possibilities. For this reason I want to encourage reader-users of this book to browse through the recipes and note for example that the "Appetizer" chapter includes many dishes that would make superb luncheon or supper fare—or—that smaller portions of some of the recipes in the "Fish" chapter would make excellent first courses.

This cook book need not be used as a rigid manual of instruction. *Just Delicious* reflects my own personal style; I know the recipes will work this way, but imaginative cooks can use them as a starting point for innovations of their own. Whether the recipes are strictly adhered to or freely interpreted, the goal for all concerned should be the same—to spice table and life with variety, and to season both "to taste" with one's own brand of *joie de vivre*.

Appetizers

Appetizers

SMOKED SALMON MOUSSE

[serves 8 to 10 as an hors-d'oeuvre]

½ pound salmon
1 cup heavy cream
juice of ½ lemon

2 tablespoons melted butter
¼ teaspoon white pepper
sliced white bread and butter

Dice the smoked salmon. Combine with the other ingredients and whirl in a blender until smooth. Chill. Mound on a small serving plate and serve on a large tray surrounded by:

Your own toast: Use slightly stale good quality white bread. Remove crusts and cut in quarters. Butter lightly on one or both sides. Bake in a 400° oven turning occasionally until browned, thoroughly dry, and crisp.

To prepare ahead of time: Both the salmon mousse and the toast can be done ahead of time. The mousse will keep in the refrigerator (tightly covered) for several days. The toast can be put in plastic bags and refrigerated—than reheated in a 350° oven and served either hot or at room temperature.

To freeze: The mousse freezes. Wrap tightly first in plastic, then in foil. Freeze the toast squares in plastic bags and reheat as directed above.

KIPPER PÂTÉ

[makes about 1½ cups pâté]

This was prompted by something quite similar that I ate at the Connaught in London.

1 pound of smoked kippers
juice of 1 large lemon

½ pound sweet butter
chopped parsley

Place kippers in a skillet. Cover with boiling water and simmer ever so gently (covered) for 10 minutes. Drain, cool, then bone and skin the kippers.

Melt butter over low heat (don't cook it!) and then whirl in the blender with the boned kippers and lemon juice. Spoon into small crocks or dishes and chill. Remove from refrigerator about half an hour before serving. Sprinkle with chopped parsley. Serve with melba toast or unsalted, unflavored crackers or rye bread. Or best of all with hot freshly made toast.

To prepare ahead of time: This can be made as much as a week ahead and kept tightly covered and refrigerated.

To freeze: This freezes. Wrap tightly first in plastic wrap and then in foil.

PÂTÉ PANGLOSS   [serves 8 to 10]

A foolproof, versatile, and delicate pâté—reminiscent of fine French foie gras.

½ pound fresh chicken livers
½ clove garlic, mashed
½ medium onion, chopped
6 tablespoons butter
¾ teaspoon salt
¼ teaspoon pepper
⅛ teaspoon thyme
⅛ teaspoon oregano
⅛ teaspoon tarragon
2 slices of firm white bread, crusts removed
½ cup light cream
2 eggs
½ teaspoon soy sauce
1 tablespoon cognac (or brandy)

Put cream and eggs in a large bowl and beat. Add bread and mash. Sauté chopped onions in the butter until tender but not browned. Add garlic and cook half a minute. Add chicken livers and cook one minute. Remove from heat and add salt, pepper, herbs, soy sauce and cognac. Add to cream mixture and stir. Whirl in a blender (about ⅓ to ½ at a time), pouring purée into a bowl. Mix well. Spoon purée into a very well greased pan (about 3¾ by 7½ by 2). Cover tightly with heavy foil and place in a baking pan. Pour boiling water into baking pan until it reaches about half way up the sides of the pâté

4

pan. Bake for about 1½ hours in a 300° oven. Cool on a rack without removing foil. Then unmold and wrap first in plastic, then in foil. Chill thoroughly.

To prepare ahead of time: This should keep in the refrigerator 5 to 10 days (depending on how well your refrigerator is working). Once you have unwrapped and sliced the pâté it should be eaten promptly. Keep unused portion wrapped and refrigerated at all times.

To freeze: This loses its delicate texture during the freezing process. Freeze only as a means of preserving the leftovers for family use.

BRANDIED AND HERBED SPECIAL
CHICKEN LIVER PÂTÉ   [makes about 4 or 5 small crocks]

1 pound fresh chicken livers	½ teaspoon pepper
2 medium-size onions,	1 bay leaf
chopped	⅛ teaspoon thyme
½ cup butter	⅛ teaspoon oregano
1 clove garlic, mashed	⅛ teaspoon tarragon
¼ cup butter	3 tablespoons cognac
1 tablespoon flour	(or brandy)
1 teaspoon salt	

Sauté the onions in the ½ cup butter with the garlic until tender, then remove from skillet. Add the ¼ cup butter to skillet and sauté the livers until almost tender. Sprinkle with flour and add the salt, pepper, bay leaf, thyme, oregano, and tarragon. Cover and simmer over low heat for about 1 or 2 minutes or until livers are cooked. Discard bay leaf. Combine liver mixture with onions. Add cognac.

Whirl mixture in the blender (about ¼ of the quantity at a time) and place in a bowl. Stir, then divide into crocks. Cover tightly and refrigerate.

To prepare ahead of time: This can be made a day or two ahead. Cover first with plastic wrap then with foil.

To freeze: Yes, this freezes beautifully. Wrap first in plastic, then in foil.

SHRIMP AND AVOCADO [serves 12 as a first course]

2 pounds of tiny bay shrimp (Icelandic type)
4 ripe avocados

1½ cups (about) of a favorite Russian dressing
salt and pepper to taste
lemon juice

Split avocados in half, then scoop out the smallest size balls possible. Place in a bowl and sprinkle with lemon juice. Cover tightly and keep refrigerated. Remove remaining avocado pulp and combine with the Russian dressing.

Place about ⅔ of the shrimp and ⅔ of the avocado balls in a large bowl. Pour the Russian dressing over them and combine with the aid of a rubber spatula (to avoid crushing the avocado). Taste for seasoning. Spoon into individual serving dishes. Top each with a decorative design made with the remaining shrimp and avocado balls. Sprinkle a little more lemon juice on the avocado. Wrap each dish tightly with plastic wrap and refrigerate until time to serve.

To prepare ahead of time: The avocado can be scooped in the early afternoon; if mixed with lemon juice and covered with plastic wrap they will keep until evening. The individual dishes can be filled, covered, and refrigerated several hours before serving.

DOROTHY WOLPERT'S EXOTIC AND DELICIOUS PAPAYA, SHRIMP, AND CURRY [serves 6]

A superb first course! I would think it equally delightful as a light luncheon dish.

3 papayas, peeled, halved, and seeded
For the curry sauce:
1 cup mayonnaise
juice of one large lime
1½ teaspoons curry powder

1 pound of tiny bay shrimp (Icelandic type)

½ teaspoon ground cumin
pinch of chili powder

Combine ingredients for curry sauce and chill. Also chill papaya and shrimp in separate containers. Just before serving divide shrimp into papaya shells and spoon curry sauce over the shrimp.

6

Note: Taste sauce for curry powder and cumin—add more if you like it spicier.

To prepare ahead of time: Curry sauce can be made the day before or in the morning—papaya can be readied in the morning. (Assemble, however, only shortly before serving.)

CANTALOUPE BASKETS WITH HONEYDEW AND PROSCIUTTO [serves 8]

4 very small cantaloupes
1 honeydew melon

½ pound thinly sliced
   prosciutto

Cut cantaloupes in half. Remove seeds and peel the outside skin so the entire half is edible. Scoop small balls from the honeydew and arrange them in the cantaloupe halves. Place on individual dishes and arrange the sliced prosciutto at the side of each cantaloupe basket. Cantaloupe and melon should be icy cold; prosciutto is best at room temperature.

To prepare ahead of time: The cantaloupe baskets and melon balls can be readied in the morning. Keep tightly wrapped in the refrigerator.

JOANNE WEINER'S MINIATURE SWEET AND SOUR CABBAGE ROLLS [makes about 70]

1 pound ground round steak
1 egg
2 tablespoons water
salt and pepper to taste
¼ teaspoon garlic salt
⅛ cup uncooked rice (rinsed)
½ medium onion, grated
3 heads of cabbage
½ medium onion, sliced

1 tablespoon vegetable shortening
⅓ cup water
salt and pepper
large can of tomatoes (need
   2 cups of tomatoes without
   the juice)
½ cup brown sugar (pack to
   measure)
¾ cup vinegar

7

Make the filling: Combine the ground round, egg, 2 tablespoons of water, salt, pepper, garlic salt, rice, grated onion and mix thoroughly.

To prepare wrappers and assemble: Remove a wide core in each head of cabbage. Fill a soup kettle ⅔ full of water and bring to a boil. Cook the cabbages for about 5 minutes or until the leaves are just wilted enough to separate easily. DO NOT OVERCOOK. (If the outer leaves are wilted but the inner part is not, replace inner part in the hot water for a few more minutes.)

Prepare roasting pan by browning the sliced ½ onion in the vegetable shortening (this can be done in the pan itself) and then adding the ⅓ cup of water. Set aside while you make the rolls.

Cut the cabbage leaves to about 4" by 4". Do not use the very heavy core part of the outer leaves. (Some of the inner leaves will be just the right size.) Do not use leaves with holes in them. Put about 1 rounded teaspoon of the meat mixture on the cabbage leaf in the middle towards the bottom. Fold the bottom up over the meat, then fold the sides in, one at a time, overlapping them, and roll up once more forming the little cabbage roll. Place in rows on the onions and water in the roasting pan. Salt and pepper each layer as completed. There should be about two layers. Over the top, if desired, add ½ cup of the extra cabbage, cut in smaller pieces.

To season: Crush tomatoes with your hands and sprinkle over the top of the rolls. Then sprinkle on the brown sugar and vinegar. Bake covered about 3 hours at 325°, then uncover and allow to brown slightly and the juice to reduce—about 30 minutes. If more juice is needed add water and salt, sugar and vinegar.

Note: The flavor can be more sweet or more sour to suit the individual but it takes about 2 to 2½ hours for the sugar and vinegar to blend.

To serve: Carefully arrange the baked rolls (rewrapping and tidying them if needed) in a shallow heatproof casserole. Heat briefly in the oven and serve hot with small plates and forks.

To prepare ahead of time: This can easily be done the day before. Arrange rolls in the heatproof casserole, cover and refrigerate. Before serving cover with foil and reheat in the oven.

To freeze: Yes, these do freeze. Arrange rolls in foil pans (or even in the casserole or casseroles that you plan to heat and serve them from) and cover and seal tightly. To use, defrost completely, cover with foil, then reheat in the oven and serve.

Special note: The three heads of cabbage sounds like a bit much, however, you will need them to make the rolls since not all the leaves are suitable. Use leftover cabbage as a family vegetable.

CRÊPES WITH SMOKED FISH DÉLICE   [enough for 8 as a first course]

In remembrance of a similar concoction eaten at La Quetsch, Paris.

8 crêpes, 6 or 7 inches in diameter (recipe follows)
2 cups boned, smoked fish (I use smoked white fish that I VERY CAREFULLY debone)

8 scant tablespoons grated Cheddar cheese
Mornay sauce (recipe follows)

Crêpes:

3 eggs
1 cup milk
¾ cup flour

4 tablespoons melted butter
⅛ teaspoon salt
additional butter for cooking crêpes

Beat eggs with salt, add flour and milk alternately. Add melted butter. Let stand for 1 hour or longer. Batter should be the consistency of heavy cream. Add more milk if necessary.

Cook crêpes with a little additional butter in a small skillet, stacking them after they have been cooked with melted butter in between; this keeps them moist. They can be cooled, wrapped in foil packages —about 8 to a package—and frozen at this point.

Mornay sauce:

4 tablespoons butter
4 tablespoons flour
2 cups milk

salt and pepper
6 tablespoons grated Parmesan

9

Melt butter, stir in flour, then gradually add milk, stirring constantly until mixture boils. Add salt and pepper and simmer slowly for about 3 or 4 minutes, stirring occasionally. Remove from heat and stir in Parmesan. Taste for seasoning then set aside.

To assemble and serve: Place ¼ cup of the boned smoked fish on each pancake, roll up and place them in a lightly greased shallow casserole. Coat with the Mornay sauce and sprinkle with the grated Cheddar. Cover with **plastic wrap** and leave at room temperature until ready to heat. At that time place in a 375° oven for about 15 minutes or until hot, bubbly, and browned on top. Don't overcook. Brown under broiler if necessary.

To prepare ahead of time: These can be completely prepared either the day before or in the morning. Cover with plastic wrap and refrigerate. About two hours before serving remove to bring them to room temperature. Proceed with the heating as directed above.

To freeze: Do not freeze these filled. The crêpes, however, can be frozen as described above in the recipe. To use, defrost and then heat them in their foil package in a low oven (about 300°) only long enough to make the crêpes flexible. This avoids the usual breaking or cracking when you try to roll them.

CRÊPES BALTIC [enough for 8 as a first course]

Inspired by a first course of the same name served to us at Au Pactole, Paris.

8 crêpes, 6 or 7 inches in diameter, see recipe on p. 9

5½ oz. can of Matjes herring filets (imported from Scandinavia)—rinsed and thoroughly drained

Wine-tarragon sauce (recipe follows)

Wine-tarragon sauce

2 tablespoons butter
2 tablespoons flour
½ cup dry white wine
1 cup light cream
1 teaspoon chopped fresh tarragon (or ¼ teaspoon dried)

salt and pepper to taste
2 teaspoons grated Parmesan
1 egg yolk
1 or 2 teaspoons chopped fresh chives

10

Melt butter, stir in flour, then gradually add wine and cream, stirring constantly until mixture boils. Reduce heat and simmer gently. Add tarragon, salt and pepper, and Parmesan. Beat egg yolk in a small bowl. Gradually pour on the hot sauce, beating while adding. Return to saucepan, add chives, and set aside.

To assemble and serve: Place two herring filets in each pancake, then roll up and place in a lightly greased shallow casserole. Spoon sauce over each rolled and filled pancake. Place casserole on upper rack of a preheated 450° oven and bake until hot and lightly browned. If desired, they can be browned additionally by placing the casserole briefly under a broiling unit. More chopped chives can be sprinkled on top before serving.

To prepare ahead of time: These can be completely prepared either the day before or in the morning. Cover with plastic wrap and refrigerate. Remove two hours before serving to bring them to room temperature. Proceed with the heating as directed above.

To freeze: Do not freeze these filled. The crêpes, however, can be frozen as mentioned in the recipe for them on p. 10. To use, defrost and then heat them in their foil package in a low oven (about 300°) only long enough to make the crêpes flexible. This avoids the usual breaking or cracking when you try to roll them.

TINY CRÊPES WITH CAVIAR AND SOUR CREAM
[serves 8 to 10 as a first course]

Crêpes (3 inches in diameter), see recipe below
1 pint sour cream, chilled

Black lumpfish caviar—about 2 teaspoons per guest (or if you are in a wildly extravagant mood serve the unsalted Beluga jewels!)

Crêpes:

3 eggs
1 cup milk
¾ cup flour

4 tablespoons melted butter
⅛ teaspoon salt
additional butter for cooking crêpes

Beat eggs with salt, add flour and milk alternately. Add melted butter. Let stand for 1 hour or longer. Batter should be the consistency of heavy cream. Add more milk if necessary.

Cook crêpes with some additional butter—if possible in that Danish iron skillet with the seven shallow indentations—otherwise do them in any skillet or on a griddle. As they are cooked brush them with melted butter and stack about 8 to 10 together. This keeps them moist. They can be cooled, wrapped in foil packages and frozen at this point.

To serve: Place crêpes overlapping in a large shallow ovenproof serving dish or casserole. Cover with foil and place in a 350° oven until hot. Do not overcook. Bring this dish to the table along with the bowls of sour cream and caviar. Serve each guest 6 to 8 of the tiny crêpes with a portion of sour cream and caviar on the side.

To prepare ahead of time: The crêpes can be cooked the day before or in the morning. Bring to room temperature, then proceed as in above recipe.

To freeze: The crêpes can be frozen as already mentioned. To use, defrost and then heat them in their foil packages in a low oven (about 300°) only long enough to make it easy to separate them. Then proceed as above.

Note: To simplify service and to surprise and delight your guests serve this as a first course in the living room. Your plates, forks, sour cream, and caviar can be there when the guests arrive. All that is needed is to bring in the hot crêpes and then listen to the hurrahs.

ONIONS "MONÉGASQUE" [serves 6 or more]

My version of what is so often found among the hors-d'oeuvre variés in the south of France.

about 4 dozen tiny pearl onions	2 teaspoons sugar
½ cup water	¼ teaspoon dried basil
⅓ cup dry white wine	1 bay leaf
¼ cup white wine vinegar	⅛ teaspoon saffron
¼ cup olive oil	⅓ cup raisins
1 teaspoon salt	1 tablespoon tomato paste

Peel onions: The easiest way is to put them in boiling water, simmer for 3 minutes, drain, then rinse in cold water. Cut off root ends and skins will slip off easily. Combine water, wine, vinegar, oil, salt, sugar, basil, bay leaf, and saffron in a saucepan and bring to a boil. Add onions, cover, and cook over moderate heat until just barely tender. Add raisins, uncover, and simmer gently for about 3 more minutes. Remove bay leaf. Stir in tomato paste and place all in a serving dish. When cool, cover and refrigerate. Serve chilled or at room temperature.

Note: Serve these along with an assortment of your choice of other cold hors-d'oeuvre, some crackers or melba toast or thinly sliced rye bread.

To prepare ahead of time: These really should be prepared at least 24 hours before serving. They will keep for 1 or 2 weeks if kept tightly covered in the refrigerator.

PÂTÉ EN BRIOCHE ÉLÉGANT   [makes 2 loaves—should serve 20 as a first course]

The memory of two magnificent pâtés in brioche—one at the Hostellerie de la Poste in Avallon, the other at La Pyramide in Vienne—never stopped haunting me. Numerous trials in my kitchen finally produced a replica that satisfied me. It is not merely a tour de force—rather it is worth every minute you devote to its creation.

Pâté:

1 pound chicken livers
1 small clove garlic, mashed
1 onion, chopped
¾ cup butter
1 ¾ teaspoons salt
½ teaspoon pepper
¼ teaspoon thyme
¼ teaspoon oregano
¼ teaspoon tarragon

4 slices of firm white bread, crusts removed
1 cup light cream
3 extra large eggs
1 teaspoon soy sauce
3 tablespoons very finely chopped truffles (optional)
2 tablespoons cognac (or brandy)

Put cream and eggs in a large bowl and beat. Add bread and mash. Sauté chopped onions in the butter until tender but not browned. Add garlic and cook half a minute. Add chicken livers and cook one minute. Remove from heat and add salt, pepper, herbs, soy sauce and cognac. Add to cream mixture and stir. Whirl in a blender (about ¼ at a time), pouring purée into a bowl. Mix well. Stir in the truffles. Spoon into two very well greased pans (each about 3¾ by 7½ by 2). Cover tightly with heavy foil and place in a baking pan. Pour boiling water into baking pan until it reaches about half way up the sides of the pâté pan. Bake for about 1½ to 2 hours in a 300° oven. Cool on racks without removing foil. Then unmold and wrap them first in plastic, then in foil. Chill thoroughly.

Brioche:

1½ packages dry yeast	1½ teaspoons salt
⅓ cup warm water	4 whole eggs
⅓ cup milk, scalded and cooled	4 egg yolks
1 cup butter, melted then cooled	5 cups sifted flour (about 21 ozs.)
¼ cup sugar	1 egg, slightly beaten, to be used later as an egg wash

Sprinkle yeast on warm water and stir until dissolved. Combine milk, butter, salt, and sugar. Stir thoroughly. Beat eggs and egg yolks together, then add milk mixture. Test to see that it is lukewarm, then combine with dissolved yeast and place in a large bowl. Add flour and beat thoroughly either with an electric dough hook—or use your hands to pull and stretch dough—or beat with a wooden spoon until dough begins to pull away from sides of bowl. Place in a greased bowl, cover, and let rise anywhere from 45 minutes to 1½ hours (depending on kitchen temperature)— but just until doubled in bulk. Knock down dough, cover and refrigerate at least 3 hours, or better, overnight. If dough seems to rise in the refrigerator after the first few hours, press it down.

To assemble and serve: Remove pâté from refrigerator a few hours before beginning to assemble so that it approaches room temperature. Divide brioche dough into two equal portions. Grease two pyrex loaf pans (5 by 8 by 2½). Take each portion of dough and divide again into two portions, but this time in the ratio of ⅓ and ⅔. Roll or pat out the two large portions and place each in the bottom of the loaf pans. Press them so that the dough reaches about half way up sides of pans. Egg wash dough but try not to drip any on the pans. Place each pâté loaf on top of brioche and lightly egg wash the pâté. Roll or pat out the smaller portions of dough and egg wash one side of each. Place these, egg washed side down, on top of pâtés and press thoroughly all around so that the top pieces join the bottom ones around the sides. Let rise anywhere from 30 minutes to 2 hours. This will depend entirely upon how cold the pâté and dough are when assembled. The loaves should almost double in bulk. Egg wash the tops. Bake in a preheated 400° oven for 10 minutes. Reduce heat and bake at 350° for about 35 additional minutes. If tops get too brown, cover lightly with foil. When well browned and firm to the touch, remove from oven. Take loaves from pans and let them cool right side up on racks. (Remember to loosen breads from pan sides with a knife before trying to remove them.) When completely cooled wrap in several layers of foil and refrigerate until time to serve. Or, if you prefer, remove several hours earlier and serve at room temperature.

Note: A heavenly and delicious way to begin! Slice the loaves in front of your guests and serve on individual plates accompanied with a chilled dry white wine.

To prepare ahead of time: Best begun at least two days before serving, for example: First day: Bake pâtés and refrigerate; make brioche dough and refrigerate. Second day: Assemble and bake loaves; chill. Party day: Serve! If kept very tightly wrapped and refrigerated these can be made a week or ten days ahead of time—once unwrapped and sliced it should be eaten promptly. Keep unused portion wrapped and refrigerated at all times.

To freeze: The pâté loses its lovely texture in the freezing process. Freeze only as a means of preserving leftovers for family use.

ARTICHAUTS FORMIDABLES [serves 8]

Rich and fattening but worth a few days of pre-party starving. It was created from my recollection of a dish at Le Choiseul, Amboise.

8 very large fresh artichokes
1 large lemon
2 dozen small fresh mushrooms
½ cup butter
1 tablespoon flour
¾ cup sour cream
salt and pepper

1 teaspoon onion powder
2 tablespoons Madeira or
    sherry
8 slices of *Paté Pangloss*
    (see recipe on p. 4)
chopped parsley

Trim artichokes of all outside tough leaves, then cut off about ⅔ of the artichoke from the top. Trim and smooth places where tough leaves were removed. (One must be both ruthless and extravagant about discarding the top ⅔ of the artichoke and about removing all tough leaves!) Place in a large pan of boiling, salted water to which you have added the juice of the lemon. Cover and cook over moderate heat until tender. Drain and cool, then using a teaspoon carefully remove all the inside choke in each artichoke bottom.

Clean and slice mushrooms. Sauté in the butter for 1 or 2 minutes. Sprinkle with the flour and stir in sour cream. Keep stirring until mixture begins to boil. Add salt, pepper, onion powder, and simmer another minute or so. Add Madeira or sherry and cook one more minute. Taste for seasoning and remove from heat.

To assemble and serve: Season insides of artichoke bottoms with a little salt and peper. Spoon in the mushroom mixture. Top each with a slice of *Paté Pangloss*. Place in a large baking pan and cover with foil. Heat in a 350° oven for 10 to 15 minutes—longer if the artichokes, mushrooms, and pâté are cold. Serve hot garnished with a sprinkling of chopped parsley.

To freeze: Only freeze these as a means of saving leftovers for family use.

EGGS IN COCOTTES WITH PÂTÉ AND MADEIRA SAUCE
[serves 8 as a first course]

We dined on something like this in the French restaurant of the Londonderry Hotel, London.

8 eggs	8 small slices of *Paté Pangloss*
butter	(see recipe on p. 4)
Madeira sauce (recipe follows)	

Madeira sauce:

1 onion, finely chopped	⅓ cup Madeira
2 carrots, finely chopped	¼ cup cornstarch
4 tablespoons butter	dissolved in ¾ cup cold
2 tablespoons tomato paste	water
3 cans undiluted beef bouillon	
(4½ cups)	

Sauté the chopped onions and carrots in the butter until tender and browned. Add tomato paste and bouillon, stir, then simmer uncovered for about 15 minutes. Strain. Thicken to desired consistency with dissolved cornstarch. Taste for seasoning and add Madeira. This makes a large amount. Freeze what you don't use.

To assemble and serve: Butter individual cocottes generously. (Or if you don't have cocottes use custard cups.) Place a slice of pâté in the bottom of each. Break an egg on top of the pâté and cover each with the Madeira sauce (2 or 3 tablespoons per egg). Place cocottes in a pan of boiling water and bake at 350° for 15 minutes or longer depending on how well cooked you like your eggs. Serve at once.

To prepare ahead of time: Both the *Paté Pangloss* and the Madeira sauce can be prepared 1 to 3 days ahead. Keep refrigerated until about 3 hours before serving—then bring to room temperature and proceed as above.

To freeze: The Madeira sauce freezes and it is convenient to have available so I suggest freezing it in 1 or 2 cup portions.

CAVIAR RED AND SALMON PINK SOUFFLÉ
ROULADE [serves 10 to 14 as a first course]

In the manner of a roulade at Carrier's restaurant, London.

9 ounces cream cheese	¼ cup butter
1 ½ cups sour cream	½ cup flour
6 ounces smoked salmon	½ teaspoon onion powder
4 ounces red caviar	¼ teaspoon salt
salt only if needed	2 cups milk
1 or 2 tablespoons finely	4 egg yolks
chopped chives	4 egg whites

Prepare pan: Grease a jelly roll pan (11 by 17) with vegetable shortening. Line with waxed paper and grease the paper.

Prepare filling: Beat cream cheese until smooth, then gradually beat in sour cream. Dice salmon. Fold in salmon and caviar. Add half the chives. Taste for salt. Chill.

Make the roulade: Melt butter, stir in flour, onion powder, and salt. Add milk and stir constantly until mixture begins to boil. Remove from heat and beat in egg yolks one at a time. Beat egg whites until stiff but not dry and fold into yolk mixture. Spread this batter in prepared pan. Bake in a 325° oven for 40 to 45 minutes or until browned on top. Remove from oven and turn out upside down on a damp towel. Remove waxed paper and cut off hard edges of the roulade. Roll up from the long side in order to obtain the longest possible roll. When completely cool unroll and spread with about ¼ to ⅓ of the filling and roll up again. Place on serving dish. Cover with plastic wrap and chill.

To serve: Frost top of roulade with a thin coating of filling and sprinkle with remaining chives. Slice and place on individual serving plates. Add a spoonful of the filling at the side of each slice. A few sprigs of watercress can be added as a garnish too.

To prepare ahead of time: The roulade can be baked and filled the day before. Keep tightly covered in the refrigerator. The extra filling should also be covered and refrigerated in a separate bowl.

HAM HOTS

Devote some of your leftover baked ham to this cause.

3 to 4 dozen bread squares
softened butter
1 pound baked ham
4 to 6 green onions, finely
    chopped

½ cup mayonnaise
¾ cup Durkee's dressing
    (don't substitute, this
    gives it a distinctive
    flavor)

Toast bread squares on one side only, then butter the other side. Set aside.

Put ham through the finest blade of your meat grinder, then combine with other ingredients. Pile small spoonfuls of the ham mixture on the buttered sides of the bread squares and place under a broiling unit until browned and very hot.

Note: The ham mixture also makes excellent sandwiches.

To prepare ahead of time: The ham mixture can be prepared several days ahead and refrigerated. The canapés can be completely assembled in the morning, covered with plastic wrap, then baked later.

To freeze: The bread squares can be frozen in plastic bags.

CARAWAY, SESAME, AND POPPY SEED PASTRIES

After gazing at the lovelies at Fauchon's in Paris.

1 cup butter
8 ounces cream cheese
2 cups unsifted flour
¼ teaspoon salt
1 egg white, slightly beaten
    with 2 tablespoons of
    cold water

caraway seeds
poppy seeds
sesame seeds

Cream butter and cream cheese. Add flour and salt and combine using your hands or a pastry blender. Wrap in plastic and chill for several hours (or longer).

Roll pastry out to about a ⅛ inch thickness and cut in 3-inch circles. Brush with the egg white mixture. Sprinkle some circles with caraway seeds, some with sesame, and some with poppy seeds. Bake at 425° for 5 minutes, reduce heat to 350° and bake until golden brown and crisp.

To prepare ahead of time: These can be made several days ahead and stored either at room temperature in airtight tins or in plastic bags in the refrigerator. Reheat in a 300° oven to crisp.

To freeze: The cream cheese pastry freezes beautifully and you may want to keep some on hand at all times for these or for pies, and so on. These pastries can also be frozen after they have been rolled and cut and seeded—either baked or unbaked. If baked, reheat to crisp. If unbaked, do not defrost but proceed with the baking as in the above recipe.

GREEN OLIVES WITH ANCHOVY BUTTER

As we remember relishing them on the patio of Le Petit Auberge de Noves near Avignon.

pitted green olives (can be purchased this way—don't use the black ripe olives for this)

½ cup butter
1½ tablespoons anchovy paste

Cream butter thoroughly with the anchovy paste. Use a small pastry bag with a small tube and fill the olives. Chill before serving.

To prepare ahead of time: The olives can be stuffed several days before your party. Keep them covered and refrigerated.

To freeze: The anchovy butter freezes.

ARTICHOKES WITH SHRIMP ... AVENUE WAGRAM

[serves 6]

6 large fresh artichokes
½ pound cooked shrimp
    (use small ones or cut
    larger ones in halves
    or thirds)

1 lemon
Russian dressing (see recipe
    below)

Trim artichokes of all outside tough leaves, then cut off ⅔ of the artichoke from the top. Trim and smooth places where leaves were removed. (This may seem wasteful, however, one must be ruthless about removing the outside leaves and discarding the top ⅔ of the artichoke!) Cook the artichokes in boiling, salted water (to which you have added the juice of the lemon) until tender. Drain thoroughly and cool. Carefully remove all of the inside choke in each and refrigerate.

Russian dressing:

1 cup mayonnaise
½ cup sour cream
⅓ cup chili sauce
2 hard-cooked eggs, chopped
juice of half a lemon

2 tablespoons chopped
    pimento olives
1 teaspoon chopped parsley
1 green onion, chopped

Combine and chill.

To assemble and serve: Combine shrimp with enough of the Russian dressing to suit your taste. Season cooked artichokes lightly with salt and pepper. Fill with the shrimp mixture and serve garnished with a little watercress.

To prepare ahead of time: The artichokes can be cooked the day before. The Russian dressing can be done several days ahead. These can be completely assembled the morning of your party, covered with plastic wrap and refrigerated until time to serve.

CRABMEAT ON TOMATO HALVES WITH GREEN OLIVES AND GREEN PEPPER RINGS, WAGRAM

[serves 12]

Crabmeat mixture
   (see recipe below)
6 large tomatoes
salt and pepper
12 green pepper rings

¾ cup chopped pimento-stuffed
   green olives
lettuce leaves

Crabmeat mixture:

8 ounces crabmeat
   (fresh or canned)
3 ounces cream cheese
¼ cup sour cream
¼ cup mayonnaise
½ teaspoon soy sauce
1 teaspoon Worcestershire
   sauce

few drops of Tabasco
salt and pepper to taste
1 large clove of garlic,
   mashed
1 green onion, finely chopped
1 teaspoon finely chopped
   parsley

Soften cream cheese, then gradually beat in sour cream and mayonnaise. Add remaining ingredients and taste for seasoning. Chill.

To assemble and serve: Cut tomatoes in half (peel them first if you like). Sprinkle lightly with salt and pepper. Place tomatoes on lettuce and top each with the crabmeat mixture. Then place a green pepper ring on each and sprinkle generously with the chopped olives.

To prepare ahead of time: The crabmeat mixture is best made the day before. These can be completely assembled several hours in advance of serving. Cover tightly with plastic wrap and refrigerate.

SUMPTUOUS SHRIMP STUFFED EGGS

[serves 12]

Recalled as part of a lunch served on a flight to Copenhagen.

½ pound tiny shrimp
   (Icelandic type)
12 hard-cooked eggs
Russian dressing (see p. 21)
mayonnaise
salt and pepper

1 teaspoon dry mustard
2 tablespoons softened
   butter
½ teaspoon Worcestershire
   sauce
few drops of Tabasco

Cut eggs in half lengthwise. Remove egg yolks and press them through a sieve, then add butter, salt and pepper, Worcestershire, Tabasco, and enough mayonnaise to moisten.

Mix shrimp with Russian dressing using enough to moisten. Taste for seasoning then fill the egg whites with the shrimp. Using a pastry tube pipe the egg yolk mixture around the rim of the egg white halves. Cover with plastic wrap and chill until time to serve.

To prepare ahead of time: Eggs can be cooked the day before. They can be completely assembled and refrigerated the morning of your party.

Note: This provides two stuffed eggs per guest. If they are among other hors-d'oeuvre 24 guests can be served.

EGGS GREEN KNIGHT [serves 8]

Modeled after a sample of one of the beauties at Fauchon's in Paris.

8 hard-cooked eggs	¼ teaspoon garlic salt
2 cups watercress (stems removed)—about 1 large bunch	1 or 2 teaspoons lemon juice
⅓ cup cream	salt and pepper to taste
¾ cup mayonnaise	tiny drop of green food color (optional)

Split eggs in half lengthwise and place cut side down on a large flat dish (or two halves on each individual dish). Whirl watercress in a blender with the cream, then combine with remaining ingredients. If using the green food color add it by dipping a toothpick into color, then into watercress dressing—thus avoiding a too vivid and unpleasant effect. Spoon sauce over eggs and serve cold with an additional garnish of watercress leaves.

To prepare ahead of time: The eggs can be cooked the day before and the watercress sauce can be prepared one or two days before. They can be assembled, covered, and refrigerated the morning of the party.

23

CELERY ROOT SALAD [makes about 2 cups]

My version of a popular member of the hors-d'oeuvre
variés in France.

1 medium to large celery root	1 teaspoon Dijon mustard
⅔ cup mayonnaise	salt to taste
1½ tablespoons lemon juice	finely chopped parsley

Peel celery root and then quickly shred into match stick pieces with
a knife—or easier—use the Mouli salad maker. Combine immediately
with the other ingredients (or celery root will turn brown). Mix
and chill. Sprinkle with chopped parsley and serve.

To prepare ahead of time: This can be made one or two days ahead.
Stir gently before serving.

RAW MUSHROOM SALAD WITH TARRAGON
[serves 4 to 8]

After something similar we were served at Au Pactole in
Paris.

1 pound fresh mushrooms	3 teaspoons tomato paste
juice of 1 lemon	2 teaspoons chopped fresh
¾ cup mayonnaise	tarragon (or ¾ teaspoon
¼ teaspoon salt (or to	of the dried)
taste)	1 tablespoon Madeira

Clean and slice mushrooms, then sprinkle with lemon juice. Combine remaining ingredients and pour over the mushrooms. Stir gently and chill until time to serve.

To prepare ahead of time: This can be done the day before or in the
morning. Don't worry if the dressing separates—just stir again and
then serve.

24

EGGS IN SALAMI BIRD NESTS
WITH RUSSIAN SALAD [serves 8]

My interpretation of an amusing first course served at
lunch on an Alitalia flight from Milan to Brussels

24 to 32 slices Italian salami
8 very tiny hard-cooked eggs (fresh quail eggs if possible,
    otherwise buy the so-called "pee-wees")
lettuce leaves
Russian salad (recipe follows)
slivers of dill pickle
2 tablespoons mayonnaise, slightly thinned with cream

Russian salad:
1 cup finely chopped celery
1 cup chopped cooked carrots, well drained
1 cup diced cooked string beans, well drained
1 cup canned petit pois, well drained
1 cup cooked, diced potatoes
2 or 3 green onions, finely chopped
1 tablespoon lemon juice
salt and pepper to taste
1 cup mayonnaise
1 tablespoon anchovy paste

Combine all ingredients and mix together gently. Taste for seasoning and chill thoroughly—if possible—overnight.

To assemble and serve: Cut salami slices into very thin match-
stick pieces. Place lettuce on individual serving plates. Place a heaping tablespoon of the Russian salad on each and flatten with a knife
or spoon. Arrange slivered salami into mock bird nests on top of
salad. Top each with an egg and coat egg very lightly with thinned
mayonnaise. Garnish top of each egg with one or two slivers of
pickle.

To prepare ahead of time: The eggs and the Russian salad can be
readied the day before. The nests can be assembled the morning of
the party if you are careful to wrap each plate with plastic wrap
and keep refrigerated until time to serve.

ELIANNE'S OEUFS EN COCOTTE

eggs	salt and pepper
softened butter	heavy whipping cream

Generously butter individual cocottes (tiny individual casseroles). Break one egg into each. Season with salt and pepper. Dot each with 1 or 2 teaspoons of butter, then spoon over each 2 tablespoons of cream. Place in a baking pan and bake 15 minutes or longer in a 350° oven, depending on how well cooked you want the eggs.

Note: Be sure to use the heaviest whipping cream you can buy. It is about as close to the French crème fraîche as we can come; our commercial sour cream is unsuitable for this dish.

BEATIFIED EGGS   [serves 6]

The point of departure for this was a gorgeous first course served at the Connaught in London.

Crabmeat mixture	salt and pepper
(recipe follows)	½ cup grated Parmesan
6 eggs	

Crabmeat mixture:

2 tablespoons butter	7½-ounce can of crabmeat
2 tablespoons flour	¼ teaspoon dry mustard
½ teaspoon salt	1 cup light cream
¼ teaspoon pepper	2 tablespoons sherry
⅛ teaspoon thyme	3 green onions, very finely
¼ teaspoon garlic powder	chopped

Melt butter, stir in flour, then add salt, pepper, thyme, garlic powder, and mustard. Add cream gradually, stirring constantly until mixture boils. Add crabmeat and heat gently for one minute. Taste for seasoning. Add sherry and green onions, simmer half a minute and remove from heat.

To assemble and serve: Place a spoonful of crabmeat mixture in each of six ovenproof shallow casseroles (approximately 1½ inches deep and about 5 inches in diameter). Separate eggs carefully: place 1 egg yolk in the center and on top of the crabmeat. Sprinkle very lightly with salt and pepper. Place all egg whites in a large bowl and beat until stiff. Spoon them in cloud-like dabs on top of each casserole, completely covering egg yolk and crabmeat. Sprinkle each with about 2 tablespoons of the grated Parmesan and bake at 450° for 8 minutes. Serve at once.

Note: The *Oeufs* we ate at the Connaught had some kind of a mushroom-lobster base—would be pleasant to try that some time too.

To prepare ahead of time: One of the glories of this superb dish is that not only is it delicious to eat and fascinating to look at, but it can mostly be done ahead. Do everything except beating the egg whites. Cover each casserole with plastic wrap and leave at room temperature. (Or if preparing in the morning, place in refrigerator until 2 hours before serving, then bring to room temperature and proceed with the egg whites.) The crabmeat mixture can be prepared the day before and kept refrigerated in a bowl.

To freeze: The crabmeat mixture can be frozen separately and used as needed.

Fish and Shellfish

Fish and Shellfish

TROUT ALL PUFFED UP   [serves 4]

> Having a shadow-like resemblance to an inflated fish at
> Chez Garin in Paris.

4 fresh trout (inside bones removed—ask your fish man to do
    this for you, but keep the head and tails intact)
½ cup dry white wine
salt and pepper
Fish stock (see below)
Halibut mousse (see below)
Special sauce (see below)

Fish stock:

½ pound fish bones (from white fish—not from salmon, etc.)	1 cup water
	¼ teaspoon thyme
	½ teaspoon salt
1 cup dry white wine	1 onion, sliced

Combine, then cook over moderate heat for 30 minutes (uncovered
part of time). Strain, then set aside for later use.

Halibut mousse:

¾ pound halibut filets	1 ⅓ cups heavy cream
1 teaspoon salt	3 egg whites
¼ teaspoon white pepper	

Dice halibut, then whirl in a blender with cream and egg whites (do
about ⅓ at a time). Combine with salt and pepper. Lacking a
blender, put fish through a meat grinder about 4 or 5 times, then
place in a mixing bowl and gradually work in cream and egg whites.
Set aside.

Special sauce:

2 tablespoons butter	salt and pepper
2 tablespoons flour	2 tablespoons tomato paste
1 ½ cups strained fish stock	¼ cup raisins (washed in
¼ cup heavy cream	hot water and drained)

Melt butter, stir in flour, then gradually add fish stock, stirring constantly until mixture comes to a boil. Add cream, salt and pepper, and tomato paste and blend. Simmer gently, uncovered, for 5 to 10 minutes. Add raisins, taste for seasoning, then simmer an additional 1 minute. Set aside.

To assemble and serve: Sprinkle each trout inside and out with salt and pepper. Fill each trout very generously with the halibut mousse and place them in a buttered shallow glass casserole or enamel pan. Pour the ½ cup dry white wine over the fish. Cover loosely with foil and place in a 400° oven for about 25 minutes or longer. (This depends on how cold the fish is). Remove fish from oven. With the aid of two large spatulas lift the trout on to a very hot serving dish and bring to table with the special sauce (that you have gently reheated while trout was baking). Serve each guest a trout on warmed large plates and spoon sauce over each serving.

To prepare ahead of time: Fish stock and special sauce can be made the day before. Halibut mousse can be prepared in the morning. Trout can be stuffed with the mousse in the morning, covered with plastic wrap and refrigerated. Bring to room temperature before baking.

To freeze: Both the fish stock and the special sauce can be frozen. Defrost completely and stir over low heat before using.

Note: Serve this as the pièce de résistance. Don't put anything else on the dinner plate! Serve a hot fresh vegetable as a first course—then the fish—then perhaps a green salad—then dessert. This is too delicate and spectacular to confuse with other distracting flavors.

TRUITE EN DEUX CHEMISES [serves 4]

A collage constructed from miscellaneous gastronomic flashbacks.

4 fresh trout (inside bones removed—but leave
    heads and tails on!)
lemon
salt and pepper
1 cup fish stock (see p. 31)
½ cup dry white wine
8 crêpes, 7 or 8 inches in diameter (see p. 9)
Crabmeat stuffing (see below)
Cream sauce (see below)
melted butter

Crabmeat stuffing:

½ onion, finely chopped	1 cup crabmeat
½ pound mushrooms,	salt and pepper
finely sliced	2 eggs yolks, beaten
¼ cup butter	

Sauté onions in the butter for a few minutes. Add mushrooms and continue cooking for about 2 or 3 minutes. Stir in crabmeat. Season. Remove from heat and beat in egg yolks.

Poaching the trout: Rub trout with a little lemon juice, then season inside and out with salt and pepper. Fill cavity of each fish with stuffing. Skewer closed. Place trout in a large shallow pyrex, enamel, or stainless steel pan (not aluminum!). Add fish stock and white wine. Cover with waxed paper, then cover tightly with foil. Bake in a preheated 400° oven for about 20 minutes. Remove from oven and drain off juices. Strain the juices, then reduce by cooking to 1 cup. Set fish aside lightly covered.

Cream sauce:

2 tablespoons butter	½ cup light cream
2 tablespoons flour	salt and pepper
1 cup fish juices (left	2 egg yolks
after poaching fish)	

Melt butter, stir in flour, then add the fish juices and cook, stirring constantly, until it boils. Add cream and simmer gently for 3 min-

33

utes. Taste for seasoning. Beat egg yolks in a bowl, then gradually beat the hot sauce into the yolks. Set aside at room temperature.

To assemble and serve: Use either individual shallow oval-shaped casseroles or one large one. Place a thin layer of prepared sauce in casseroles, then place stuffed trout on this. Next spoon a little sauce over each trout. Place one crêpe around each trout but let heads and tails remain uncovered. Spoon more sauce over the crêpes. Place second crêpe directly over the first. Brush with melted butter. Place trout, uncovered, in the upper level of a 400° oven just long enough to heat completely. Do not overcook. This will take anywhere from 10 to 25 minutes depending on whether or not the fish have been refrigerated.

To prepare ahead of time: This can be completely prepared and assembled either the day before or in the morning. Keep covered and refrigerated but bring to room temperature before proceeding with the final heating.

To freeze: Both crêpes (see p. 9) and fish stock (see p. 31) are marvelous convenience items to have on hand in the freezer. Freezing the assembled dish is not recommended except as a way of preserving leftovers for family moments at table.

TWO WHITEFISH AVENUE WAGRAM [serves 8]

Originally prepared in Paris with two daurades.

2 whole large whitefish	4 tablespoons oil
6 shallots, chopped	½ cup dry white wine
2 cloves garlic, chopped	¼ cup melted butter (or more)
salt and pepper	2 tablespoons chopped parsley

Season fish inside and out with salt and pepper. Combine chopped shallots and garlic and place half of this in the cavity of each fish. Rub outside of each fish with oil and place them in a very large baking pan (glass, enamel, or stainless steel). Pour in wine. Bake at 400°, basting occasionally, for about 45 minutes. Remove from oven. Pour butter over fish, sprinkle with parsley and serve at once.

34

QUENELLES FAVORITES

Delicate pink sauce
 (see below)
1 pound halibut filets
2 ⅓ cups heavy whipping
 cream

1 ½ teaspoons salt
¼ teaspoon white pepper
4 egg whites

Delicate pink sauce:
¼ cup butter
¼ cup flour
2 cups fish stock
 (see p. 31)

½ cup cream
2 tablespoons tomato paste
salt and pepper to taste
3 tablespoons sherry

Melt butter, stir in flour. Remove from heat and when bubbling has stopped add fish stock. Return to moderate heat and stir until mixture begins to boil. Reduce heat and add cream, tomato paste, and seasoning. Simmer one minute. Add sherry and remove from heat. Set aside.

To make quenelles: Dice halibut. Purée in a blender with the cream using about ¼ of the amount at a time. Place in a large bowl and beat in salt and pepper. Beat egg whites only until barely stiff, then fold into the fish. Form into quenelles (shaping them with two tablespoons) and poach in salted simmering water. They should be cooked in 8 to 10 minutes. (Taste one!) Drain and set aside covered with plastic wrap until time to serve. Then place in a buttered dish, cover with foil and heat in a 350° oven (only until hot). Serve with the sauce. Or alternately, cover with the sauce and heat in the oven in the sauce.

To prepare ahead of time: The quenelles and sauce can be made the day before. Keep refrigerated but bring to room temperature before the final heating.

To freeze: The quenelles and the sauce both freeze well. Freeze separately—the quenelles in plastic bags and the sauce in another container.

SOLE WITH AVOCADO AND MUSHROOM STUFFING

[serves 8]

16 small filets of sole (or
    8 extra large ones)
lemon
¼ pound fresh mushrooms,
    chopped
6 green onions, finely chopped
4 tablespoons butter

2 tablespoons flour
1 tomato, chopped
1 large ripe avocado, mashed
½ cup dry white wine
½ cup fish stock (or cream)
salt and pepper to taste
2 egg yolks

Sauté mushrooms and green onions in the butter for 2 to 3 minutes. Sprinkle with the flour and stir. Add tomato and avocado and stir again. Add wine, fish stock, and seasonings and stir constantly until mixture comes to a boil. Reduce heat and simmer for about 3 minutes. Beat egg yolks and add, stirring well over low heat until mixture thickens. Remove from heat and set aside until time to use.

Season sole with salt, pepper, and a little lemon juice. Place 8 of the filets in a large baking pan. Place half the stuffing on them. Place remaining filets on top of stuffing and then a final layer of stuffing on top of those. Bake at 400° for about 25 minutes or until fish flakes easily. Serve very hot directly from your casserole.

To prepare ahead of time: This can be assembled in the morning, covered and refrigerated. Bring to room temperature, then proceed with the baking as directed above.

RED SNAPPER WITH TOMATO,
ONION, AND GREEN OLIVES

[serves 4]

4 red snapper filets
salt and pepper
1 onion, chopped

2 tablespoons butter
2 cups canned tomatoes, mashed
½ cup pitted green olives

Place chopped onion and butter in a shallow ovenproof casserole (pyrex or enamel) and season lightly with salt and pepper. Place in a 400° oven and bake for 10 minutes, stirring once or twice. Add tomatoes and bake an additional 10 minutes. Season fish with salt and pepper and place in the casserole. Spoon tomato-onion mixture over fish. Return to oven and bake approximately 15 to 20 minutes, basting once. Remove from oven, scatter olives on top. Return to oven for about 5 minutes—long enough to heat—and serve hot from the casserole.

To prepare ahead of time: The tomato-onion mixture can be readied in the morning. Add fish shortly before serving and proceed as above.

PONT ALMA FILETS OF SOLE [serves 4]

Animated by a noble fish dish we ate in a restaurant near the Pont Alma in Paris.

8 large filets of sole	1 ½ cups fish stock (see p. 31)
salt and pepper	*Special sauce* (see below)
Mushroom filling (see below)	¼ pound tiny shrimp

Mushroom filling:

¼ pound fresh mushrooms	¼ teaspoon salt
2 tablespoons butter	⅛ teaspoon pepper
½ onion, finely chopped	1 ½ tablespoons flour
⅛ teaspoon thyme	½ cup sour cream

Chop mushrooms as finely as possible. Melt butter, then sauté chopped onion until lightly browned. Add mushrooms, thyme, salt, pepper, and cook about 5 minutes, stirring frequently. Sprinkle with flour and stir. Reduce heat and add sour cream. Cook, stirring constantly, until thickened. Cool.

Poaching the sole: Season filets of sole with salt and pepper. Spread mushroom filling on four of the filets, then top them sandwich style with the remaining four. Pour ½ cup fish stock into a large shallow pyrex or enamel casserole. Place fish in casserole. Cover with foil and poach in a 400° preheated oven for about 20 to 25 minutes. Remove fish using a large spatula to another casserole and cover lightly with plastic wrap while preparing sauce.

Special sauce:

2 tablespoons butter	2 egg yolks
2 tablespoons flour	¼ cup cream
1 ½ cups fish stock (use juices remaining from poaching fish plus additional from stock already prepared)	1 tomato, peeled and seeded, then chopped
	salt and pepper to taste

Melt butter, stir in flour, then add fish stock. Cook, stirring constantly, until mixture boils. Reduce heat and cook uncovered until sauce reduces and thickens. Beat egg yolks with cream and then add hot sauce to egg yolk mixture while beating. Return to sauce-pan and cook over very low heat only until sauce is hot and thickens a little more. Don't let this boil after egg has been added. Stir in tomato and taste for seasoning.

To assemble and serve: Spoon sauce and shrimp over the poached fish. Place in the upper part of a 400° oven until hot and lightly browned. Don't overcook! (If desired it can be browned additionally under a broiling unit.) Serve at once.

To prepare ahead of time: This can be completely assembled the day before or in the morning. Cover with plastic wrap and refrigerate. Bring to room temperature about 2 hours before serving, then proceed with the final heating.

To freeze: This can be frozen (before the final heating). Defrost completely, then proceed as directed in the above recipe.

REX SOLE IN RED WINE WITH A WHITE WHIPPED BUTTER SAUCE [serves 6]

My version of an enigmatic delicacy served to us at the Hotel de la Poste in Beaune.

6 large rex soles	¼ teaspoon pepper
salt and pepper	½ teaspoon salt
2 cups dry red wine	4 very large shallots, thinly sliced
2 cups water	
2 large cloves garlic, split	*White whipped butter sauce*
1 small onion, chopped	(see below)

38

White whipped butter sauce:

- 1 tablespoon finely chopped shallots
- ¼ cup dry white wine
- 2 tablespoons white wine vinegar
- ¼ teaspoon salt
- ⅛ teaspoon pepper
- ¾ pound chilled butter, thinly sliced

Cook chopped shallots, wine, vinegar, salt, and pepper together until reduced to about 1 ½ tablespoons, then gradually whip in the sliced chilled butter. Use a whisk for this. It should have the texture of Hollandaise. Set aside until ready to use. Some culinary experts say that this must be made the last minute—just before serving. I find, however, that if you whip it again before using—either at room temperature or over barely simmering water—it can be done in advance. Do not, however, overheat—barely warm is sufficient for the sauce if the fish is hot and is served on very hot plates.

To prepare fish: Cook red wine, water, garlic, onion, pepper, and salt together uncovered for 15 minutes. Strain. Season fish lightly with salt and pepper and place in a large shallow casserole. Pour strained wine mixture over fish and top with sliced shallots. Poach in a 400° oven for about 15 to 20 minutes.

To serve: Remove fish from poaching liquid and place on very hot dinner plates. Top each with some of the sliced shallots and serve each with a generous spoonful of white butter sauce. Superb!

To prepare ahead of time: The white butter sauce can be prepared one or two days ahead of time. Keep tightly covered and refrigerated. Bring to room temperature before using, then proceed as directed in the recipe.

To freeze: The white butter sauce can be frozen. Defrost overnight in the refrigerator. Bring to room temperature before using, then proceed as directed in the recipe.

SALMON WITH A CHAMPAGNE SAUCE [serves 6]

Encouraged by some exceptional salmon served to us at
La Pyramide in Vienne.

6 salmon filets
salt and pepper
sprig of parsley
1 cup of champagne
1 cup drained canned
     tomatoes, chopped
½ pound mushrooms, sliced

2 tablespoons butter
2 tablespoons flour
½ teaspoon fresh chopped
     tarragon (or ⅛ teaspoon
     of dried)
1 cup heavy cream
finely chopped parsley

Season salmon lightly with salt and pepper. Place in an ovenproof pyrex or enamel casserole. Add champagne, parsley sprig, tomatoes, and sliced mushrooms. Cover with foil and poach in a 350° oven for 25 to 30 minutes, or until fish flakes easily. Do not overcook. Remove from oven and lift fish into another casserole (one that you can heat and serve from). Remove mushrooms and scatter over fish. Discard parsley and cook remaining juices until reduced to one cup. Strain and set aside.

Melt butter, stir in flour, then add the fish juices you have reduced to 1 cup and cook, stirring, until mixture comes to a boil. Add cream and simmer gently for several minutes. Add tarragon and taste for seasoning. Spoon sauce over fish. Place in a 375° oven until hot and bubbly. If desired the top can be browned under the broiling unit. Sprinkle with parsley and serve.

To prepare ahead of time: This can be prepared the day before or in the morning up to the point of the final heating. Cover fish with sauce and refrigerate. Bring to room temperature, then proceed as in above recipe.

To freeze: Yes, this can be frozen. Defrost overnight in the refrigerator. Bring to room temperature several hours before serving, then proceed as directed above.

SALMON STEAKS WITH SOUR CREAM, GREEN PEPPERS, AND SHRIMP

[serves 10]

10 fresh salmon steaks	2 cups sour cream
salt and pepper	2 onions, sliced wafer thin
lemon	3 green peppers, sliced in
2 tablespoons butter	rings
2 tablespoons flour	½ pound bay shrimp
1 teaspoon salt	(Icelandic type)
½ teaspoon pepper	3 tablespoons butter

Season salmon steaks with salt, pepper, and lemon juice. Place in two large buttered ovenproof casseroles (pyrex, enamel, or stainless steel). Melt butter, stir in flour, and then add the 1 teaspoon of salt and the ½ teaspoon of pepper. Add sour cream and stir until mixture comes to a boil. Remove from heat.

Arrange about half the onion slices over the fish in both casseroles, then spoon on sauce, then top with the rest of the onion and all the green pepper rings. Cover with foil and bake in a 425° oven for 10 minutes. Remove foil and continue baking for about 15 to 20 additional minutes.

Heat bay shrimp in the 3 tablespoons of butter (but do not cook them or they will toughen). Sprinkle on top of salmon and serve at once from the casseroles.

To prepare ahead of time: This can be assembled in the morning with the sauce, onions, and green peppers, then baked before serving. If salmon has been refrigerated it will take longer to bake.

SALMON STEAKS WITH ANCHOVY BUTTER AND ANCHOVIES

[serves 6]

6 fresh salmon steaks	1 tablespoon anchovy paste
salad oil	18 flat anchovies, well drained
salt and pepper	and separated
¼ cup butter	

Whip or cream butter and anchovy paste together and set aside. Season salmon very lightly with salt and pepper and place in an oiled baking pan. Sprinkle each steak with a little oil, then broil salmon to your taste. Remove from oven and spread some of the anchovy butter on each and garnish each serving with 3 of the anchovy filets. Serve at once.

To prepare ahead of time: Anchovy butter will keep several weeks in the refrigerator.

To freeze: The anchovy butter freezes.

LOBSTER TAILS WITH A SOUR CREAM GARLIC SAUCE
[serves 6]

very small Australian lobster
    tails (2 to 4 per person
    depending on size)
salt and pepper
butter

lemon juice
chopped parsley
Sour cream garlic sauce
    (see recipe below)

Sour cream garlic sauce:

1 cup sour cream
1 clove garlic, mashed
3 green onions, finely chopped
salt and pepper to taste

2 or 3 tablespoons red
    wine vinegar
    (or lemon juice)

Combine all ingredients and chill. Make this at least several hours before serving—better if chilled overnight.

To prepare and serve: Split lobster tail shells lengthwise along the curved side and lift meat up on top of the shells. Season with salt and pepper and sprinkle with melted butter. Place in a pan and bake at 500° for 10 to 20 minutes (depending on size) and baste once or twice with some additional butter. Remove from oven and spoon on more melted butter that has been seasoned with lemon juice. Sprinkle with chopped parsley and serve. Chilled sour cream garlic sauce should be passed to guests in a separate bowl.

DILLED SHRIMP NEREUS WITH DILL-WATERCRESS
SAUCE [serves 6]

I originally prepared this dish with langoustines in Paris;
it is equally delicious with jumbo shrimp.

Dill-watercress sauce
  (see below)
3 pounds of green jumbo
  shrimp
4 quarts water
⅓ cup salt
4 garlic cloves
2 large onions, sliced
juice of 2 lemons
1 cup mild vinegar

4 celery stalks
2 teaspoons Worcestershire
  sauce
¼ teaspoon thyme
¼ teaspoon sweet basil
2 bay leaves
sprig of parsley
1½ cups of fresh dill
few drops of Tabasco

Dill-watercress sauce:

¾ cup chopped watercress
¼ cup finely chopped fresh
  dill
2 tablespoons chopped parsley
1 cup mayonnaise

1 cup sour cream
juice of 1 lemon
salt and pepper
½ teaspoon garlic
  powder

Combine all ingredients and chill several hours—better overnight.

To cook and serve: Remove mud veins from shrimp but leave them
in their shells. Combine ingredients other than shrimp in a very large
cooking pot and cook over moderate heat for 30 minutes. Strain,
then return liquid to the large pot. Shortly before serving bring to a
boil again, add shrimp and cook gently for about 2 minutes (after
shrimp has come to a boil)—only until shrimp are pink. Do not overcook and do not let the liquid boil hard—just a simmer or the shrimp
will toughen. Drain and serve at once if you plan to eat them hot.
(Or chill and serve cold.) The dill-watercress sauce should be passed
in a separate bowl.

To prepare ahead of time: The dill-watercress sauce can be made
several days ahead. The seasoned broth for the shrimp can be cooked
and strained in the morning. If shrimp are to be served cold, cook
them the day before or in the morning.

Note: This is strictly for informal eating—guests must be willing to
shell their own shrimp at table.

SCALLOPED SCALLOPS [serves 4 to 6]

1 large onion, finely
   chopped
olive oil
1½ pounds tiny scallops
   (if only large ones
   are available, cut in
   halves or quarters)
salt and pepper

flour
2 cloves garlic, mashed
⅔ cup dry white wine
2 cups chopped tomatoes
   (fresh or canned—but
   not too much liquid)
4 tablespoons bread crumbs
2 tablespoons chopped parsley

Sauté onion for 2 or 3 minutes in about 1 tablespoon of olive oil. Remove from skillet. Season scallops with salt and pepper, then dust with flour and shake off excess. Sauté scallops in 2 tablespoons of olive oil until lightly browned. Sprinkle with half the cooked onion and add wine. Cover and simmer gently for about 1 minute. Remove from heat—it is important not to overcook them. Remove scallops to a plate or bowl and set aside.

Add about 2 more tablespoons of olive oil to skillet and heat until sizzling. Add tomatoes and stir vigorously. Add remaining onions and garlic and reduce heat quickly to a simmer. Taste for seasoning and cook for 1 or 2 minutes. Remove from heat and set aside.

To assemble and serve: Place tomato mixture in the bottom of a shallow casserole. Top with scallops. Sprinkle with breadcrumbs and parsley. Place uncovered in a 400° oven only until very hot—about 10 minutes or a bit longer if food is at room temperature. Serve directly from the casserole.

To prepare ahead of time: This can be completely assembled the day before or in the morning. Bring to room temperature a few hours before serving, then proceed with the heating as directed above.

CLAMS AND MUSHROOMS WITH SPAGHETTI

[serves 4 to 6]

1 onion, finely chopped
¼ cup oil
2 cloves garlic, mashed
¾ pound fresh mushrooms, sliced
1 8-ounce can tomato sauce
2 cups canned tomatoes
1 teaspoon salt (about)

¼ teaspoon pepper
¼ teaspoon sugar
¼ teaspoon oregano
3 7-ounce cans minced clams
1 pound thin spaghetti
3 tablespoons butter
freshly grated Parmesan

Sauté onion for a few minutes in the oil, then add garlic and mushrooms and continue cooking a few additional minutes, stirring occasionally. Add tomato sauce, canned tomatoes (well mashed), salt, pepper, sugar, oregano, and the juice from the clams. (Do not add clams until shortly before serving.) Simmer for about an hour. Taste for seasoning. (If sauce seems too thin you can thicken it very lightly with a mixture of two teaspoons of flour kneaded with two teaspoons of softened butter.) Add clams, heat (but do not boil) and serve with the spaghetti.

To cook spaghetti: Cook spaghetti in a very large quantity of salted boiling water to which you have added a tablespoon of oil. Cook only until barely tender—*al dente*—then drain and toss with the 3 tablespoons of butter.

Serve on hot plates with a generous portion of sauce on each serving of the spaghetti. Pass freshly grated Parmesan cheese.

To prepare ahead of time: The sauce can be made several days ahead and kept refrigerated. Reheat gently so as not to toughen the clams.

To freeze: The sauce can be frozen. Defrost, then reheat gently so as not to toughen the clams.

45

Poultry

Poultry

CHICKEN CHARIVARI [serves 12]

6 pounds chicken breasts
   and thighs
salt and pepper
flour
½ cup butter
½ pound mushrooms, sliced
½ package Lipton's dried
   onion soup
2 cups chicken stock

2 cups dry red wine
⅛ teaspoon marjoram
⅛ teaspoon thyme
2 tablespoons tomato paste
½ cup Marsala
¼ cup cognac
1 tablespoon cornstarch
2 tablespoons cold water

Season chicken with salt and pepper. Dust with flour and sauté in butter until browned. As you finish browning pieces place them in a large roasting pan or casserole with a cover. Sauté mushrooms in the same skillet, adding more butter if necessary. Add dried onion soup, chicken stock, red wine, marjoram, thyme, tomato paste, Marsala, and cognac. Cover and bake at 350° for about 40 minutes or until tender. Remove from oven and place chicken on a hot serving platter (or another casserole). Dissolve cornstarch in cold water and add to sauce, stirring constantly until it boils. Pour over chicken and serve.

To prepare ahead of time: This can be done the day before or in the morning. Don't overcook chicken—it will cook a little more in the reheating.

To freeze: Yes this can be frozen. Defrost completely, then reheat gently. (Don't overcook the chicken the first time since it will cook a bit more in the reheating.)

COQ AU VIN FOR TWELVE

6 pounds of chicken breasts
and thighs
⅓ pound bacon
1 pound fresh mushrooms,
sliced
24 small boiling onions, peeled

2 tablespoons cornstarch
4 cups dry red wine
¼ cup tomato paste
1 garlic clove, mashed
salt and pepper to taste

Cook bacon in a large skillet until crisp, then remove bacon but leave the drippings. Sauté the mushrooms briefly in the bacon drippings, then place them in a large roasting pan with a tight-fitting cover. Brown chicken pieces in same skillet, adding them to roasting pan as they are browned. Boil onions for 2 or 3 minutes, drain and add to chicken.

Remove all fat from skillet except for 2 tablespoons, then add the cornstarch and stir. Add all remaining ingredients and stir until sauce comes to a boil. Pour over chicken. Cover and bake 40 minutes or longer—just until tender. Remove from oven and transfer to another casserole. Pour sauce over chicken and sprinkle with crumbled bacon.

To prepare ahead of time: This can be cooked the day before or in the morning but don't overcook. It will cook a little more in the re-heating.

To freeze: This can be frozen. Do not overcook. Defrost and then heat slowly in a 325° oven until very hot and tender.

POULET RUE PONCELET   [serves 4]

Named after a favorite market street in Paris—prepared in an apartment nearby.

1 large roasting chicken
(5 pounds or more)
¼ cup softened butter
salt and pepper
1 onion, cut in quarters
1 teaspoon dried rosemary
garlic powder

8 tiny fresh carrots (or large
ones cut into small ones)
8 small boiling onions, peeled
8 small new potatoes, (or
large ones cut into small
ones)
½ cup sweet vermouth

Rub outside of chicken with softened butter. Season inside and out with salt, pepper, rosemary, and garlic powder. Place quartered onion inside chicken. Place in a heavy casserole with a tight-fitting cover (the enamel-iron type is perfect). Surround with the carrots and onions. Cover and place in a 450° oven. Bake for 1 hour and 15 minutes. Do not remove cover during this time. While chicken is roasting boil and drain the potatoes. Remove chicken from oven and add the sweet vermouth. Add potatoes and baste. Return to oven for about 10 to 15 minutes, basting once. Bring to table, then carve and serve.

To prepare ahead of time: The vegetables can be peeled and readied in the morning—even the potatoes can be boiled and drained. The chicken can be seasoned and placed in its casserole. In the evening proceed with the cooking as directed above.

POULET EN ROUGE [serves 12]

12 large chicken breasts	1 tablespoon chopped parsley
salt and pepper	½ teaspoon dried sweet basil
flour	1½ cups tomato purée
½ cup butter	1 teaspoon salt
1 onion, finely chopped	¼ teaspoon pepper
1 clove garlic, mashed	2 cups chicken stock
2 tablespoons oil	¼ cup Marsala (or sherry)
2 carrots, finely chopped	

Season chicken breasts with salt and pepper. Dust with flour and sauté in butter until lightly browned. Place them in a large casserole.

While you are browning the chicken (or sometime earlier) make the sauce: Sauté onion and garlic in the oil for a few minutes. Add remaining ingredients and simmer for about 45 minutes. Pour over chicken, cover and bake in a 350° oven for about 40 minutes or until chicken is tender.

To prepare ahead of time: This can be prepared the day before or in the morning. If so, be sure not to overcook the chicken since it will cook more in the reheating.

To freeze: Yes it does freeze. If so, be sure not to overcook before freezing; it will cook a little more during the reheating.

HONEY, ORANGE, GINGER, SOY CHICKEN [serves 4]

2 large frying chickens,
   split in halves
¼ cup oil
¾ cup soy sauce
1 cup honey

grated rind of 1 orange
juice of 2 oranges
1 tablespoon grated fresh
   ginger (or finely minced)
1 clove garlic, mashed

Place chicken skin side down in a baking pan. Combine remaining ingredients and pour ¾ of this mixture over chicken. Bake 1 hour at 350° basting occasionally. Turn chicken, pour over remaining sauce, and bake approximately ½ hour longer, basting several times.

To prepare ahead of time: This can be prepared in the morning. Leave at room temperature covered with plastic wrap. Reheat in a 350° oven, basting frequently, only until very hot.

Note: Excellent fare the next day served cold.

GARGANTUA'S GIGOTINES [serves 12 or more]

Modeled after a gigantic gigotine of duck served at the Auberge Rennequin in Paris. I suggest you divide portions in half for the faint-hearted.

12 whole (double) chicken
   breasts (boned but skin
   left on)
salt and pepper
½ cup melted butter
36 dried prunes, steamed
   and then pitted
36 tiny onions, cooked

3 cups chicken stock
4 tablespoons cornstarch
   dissolved in ½ cup cold
   water
½ cup Madeira (or sherry)
chopped parsley
Veal-pork forcemeat
   (see below)

Veal-pork forcemeat:

¾ pound lean veal
¾ pound lean pork
¼ pound fresh pork fat
1 onion, finely chopped
¼ cup butter
¼ cup port
⅓ cup sherry

2 teaspoons salt (about)
½ teaspoon pepper
1 clove garlic, mashed
½ teaspoon thyme
¼ teaspoon oregano
¼ teaspoon tarragon
2 eggs, slightly beaten

52

Grind veal, pork, and pork fat together three times (or ask the butcher to do this). Sauté chopped onion in butter until tender but not brown. Combine with meat, add remaining ingredients and beat with a large wooden spoon.

To prepare gigotines: Open chicken breasts with the skin side down. Season with salt and pepper. Place a large spoonful of the forcemeat on each. Roll up and skewer. Place in a large shallow baking pan—don't crowd them—and brush each one with melted butter. If necessary, use two pans. Roast at 350° (uncovered), basting frequently, until browned and tender—about 1 to 1½ hours. Arrange gigotines on a large heatproof platter (or two) and remove skewers. Spoon off all remaining fat from original baking pan, then add chicken stock to pan and cook over moderate heat to deglaze. Strain into a saucepan and gradually thicken to desired consistency with the dissolved cornstarch. (Stir while adding the cornstarch mixture until it boils.) Add Madeira and simmer a minute.

Pour some of the sauce on each gigotine. Alternate prunes and onions around them. Return to oven just long enough to be certain that everything is hot. Sprinkle with parsley and serve. Pass extra sauce separately.

To prepare ahead of time: The prunes and onions can be prepared the day before. The forcemeat can be combined the day before and refrigerated. The gigotines can be cooked in the early afternoon. If so, cover with plastic wrap and leave at room temperature. Reheat in a 350° oven, basting occasionally with some of the sauce.

CHICKEN BOUNTIFUL [serves 8 to 10]

2 large frying chickens (cut into serving pieces)	4 onions, sliced
salt and pepper	3 tablespoons of good quality sweet Hungarian paprika
flour	2 cups chicken stock
½ cup butter	2 cups sour cream

Season chicken with salt and pepper. Dust with flour and brown in butter. Place pieces in a casserole as they are browned, sprinkling each with a little of the paprika. Sauté onions in same skillet until tender, then add the chicken stock and 1 cup of the sour cream. Pour all over chicken. Cover and bake about 40 minutes or until tender. Remove from oven. Add the remaining 1 cup of sour cream and stir into the sauce. Taste for seasoning. Return to oven and bake only until hot.

To prepare ahead of time: This can be prepared the day before. Refrigerate but bring to room temperature before reheating. After it has been heated stir the sauce before serving.

To freeze: This does freeze. Defrost completely. Stir sauce after reheating.

CITIFIED "COUNTRY CAPTAIN" CHICKEN [24 servings]

Pretty and especially appropriate for a buffet dinner.

5 large onions, finely chopped	6 cups canned tomatoes
1¼ cups butter	(2 no. 2½ cans),
7 green peppers, finely chopped	well mashed
2 large bunches of parsley, chopped (use tops only)	24 large chicken breasts
	salt and pepper
	flour
2 large cloves garlic, mashed	oil or vegetable shortening
salt (about 2 to 3 teaspoons)	chicken stock (about 1 cup)
1 teaspoon black pepper	2 cups raisins, soaked in hot
2 teaspoons mace	water, then drained
4 teaspoons curry powder	3 cups almonds, toasted

Sauté onions in the butter, stirring frequently, until lightly browned. Add green pepper and continue cooking about 5 more minutes. Add chopped parsley, garlic, salt, pepper, mace, curry, and stir again. Add tomatoes and simmer, stirring occasionally, until mixture thickens somewhat (about 30 minutes). Taste for seasoning and set aside.

Season chicken breasts with salt and pepper, dust with flour, then sauté in oil or vegetable shortening until well browned. Place them in a large roasting pan (or two) and cover with prepared sauce. If sauce seems too thick add some of the chicken stock. Cover tightly and bake at 325° for 30 or 40 minutes—until tender but not overcooked. Arrange chicken breasts on a very large hot serving platter. Spoon sauce over chicken. Sprinkle with prepared raisins and almonds and serve with hot steamed white rice.

To prepare ahead of time: This can be cooked the day before or in the morning. Be sure not to overcook since it will cook more in the reheating. Add almonds and raisins just before serving.

To freeze: Cook and freeze but without the almonds and raisins. Do not overcook since it will cook more in the reheating.

CHICKEN KIEV MODERNIZED [serves 4]

4 large chicken breasts, boned, skinned and flattened
salt and pepper
½ cup butter, formed into 4 finger-size pieces
flour

1 egg beaten with 1 tablespoon of water
fine white bread crumbs
watercress sprigs
baked cherry tomatoes (see recipe on p. 99)

Make your own bread crumbs (the commercial ones brown too quickly) by whirling stale white bread—crusts removed—in blender.

Season chicken breasts with salt and pepper. Place one of the butter-fingers in each, turn in sides, then roll each one up and chill.

Dust each chicken roll in flour, dip in egg mixture, then roll in the bread crumbs. Place on a waxed paper lined tray and chill again.

Just before serving fry in deep fat (at about 350° temperature) for 7 to 10 minutes and serve at once. Garnish plates with watercress and cherry tomatoes.

To prepare ahead of time: Butter-fingers and bread crumbs can be done the day before. Chicken rolls can be completed up to the point of frying in the morning.

To freeze: White bread crumbs can be kept on hand in the freezer.

Note: These are delicious and not difficult to prepare. By keeping the dinner plate simple (cherry tomatoes can be baked while the chicken is being cooked) the chicken Kiev cooking can be concentrated on and served at its spectacular best.

ONE BASTE DUCKLING WITH THREE FRUITS

[serves 4 generously]

2 Long Island ducklings
3 onions
2 celery stalks, cut in pieces
salt and pepper
2 cups duck stock (make
    it from the necks,
    giblets, and wing tips
    cooked in chicken broth)
grated rind of 1 orange

juice of 2 oranges
grated rind of 1 lemon
juice of ½ lemon
2 tablespoons cornstarch
⅓ cup currant jelly
2 fresh peaches, peeled
    and quartered
4 fresh plums, quartered
1 cup fresh seedless grapes

Remove excess fat from the ducklings. Season them inside and out with salt and pepper. Stuff each with a quartered onion and some celery. Place in a roasting pan with an onion (left whole). Using a fork prick the skin of the ducklings so that the fat will be released. Cover pan with roasting pan cover (or with heavy foil). Place in a 350° oven and roast for 1 hour and 30 minutes. *Do not uncover* during this time.

Remove pan from oven, discard the onion, and siphon off all the fat that has accumulated. (Save the fat for another purpose—pâtés, sautéing livers, etc.) Heat the oven to 425°. Now—prick the skin of the ducklings again very thoroughly with a fork. Place ducklings back in oven—this time UNCOVERED. Roast for 20 minutes. Do not baste or open oven during this period.

Remove ducklings to a large platter (ovenproof). Discard any additional fat that has accumulated in the roasting pan. Strain duck stock and add to pan. Bring to a boil, scraping all the good brown bits that have stuck to the pan into the stock. Strain into a saucepan. Dissolve cornstarch in the orange and lemon juice and add the grated rinds. Add this to the mixture in the saucepan along with the currant jelly and bring to a boil, stirring constantly. Reduce heat and simmer 2 minutes. Add all the prepared fruit to this sauce and heat 1 or 2 minutes—you do not want to cook the fruit!

To serve: Remove all the fruit from the sauce and arrange it around the ducklings. (The ducklings can be kept warm in a 300° oven while you are preparing sauce.) Bring to table, carve or cut with a poultry scissors, giving each guest some of the fruit with the duck-

56

ling. Pour generous spoonfuls of the sauce over both the duckling and the fruit.

To prepare ahead of time: The duckling can be completely cooked early in the day and the sauce prepared. Keep at room temperature loosely covered with plastic wrap. Shortly before serving place ducklings in the upper part of the oven (preheated to 400°) and heat for about 15 to 20 minutes. While this is heating, reheat sauce, add fruit, and proceed as directed in the recipe.

GAME HENS WITH RICE AND WATERCHESTNUT STUFFING
[serves 12]

12 game hens
Rice and waterchestnut
stuffing (see below)
1 cup soy sauce
½ cup honey
2 tablespoons grated
fresh ginger

¾ cup stock (make this
from the necks and giblets
of the game hens)
1 or 2 cloves garlic, mashed
¼ cup oil

Rice and waterchestnut stuffing:

1½ cups uncooked rice
1 large onion, finely chopped
1 green pepper, finely chopped
¼ cup butter

salt and pepper to taste
1 small can of waterchestnuts,
drained, rinsed, drained
again, then thinly sliced

Cook rice until barely tender. Drain, then chill. Sauté onion in the butter until tender but not browned. Add green pepper and cook, stirring, for another minute or two. Add salt and pepper, then stir in waterchestnuts. Add this mixture to the rice and mix well.

To prepare game hens: Season game hens inside and out with salt and pepper. Stuff with the rice and waterchestnut stuffing and place them in two large shallow roasting pans. Rub outside of hens with a little oil. Place in a 400° oven for about 15 minutes. (Combine remaining ingredients and stir them together for about 1 minute over low heat. Use this as a baste for the hens.) Reduce oven to 375° and bake and baste for about an hour or an hour and a half longer—or until hens are tender.

57

Note: Try serving these with Chinese style asparagus (see p. 92).

To prepare ahead of time: The rice and waterchestnut stuffing can be prepared the day before—bring to room temperature before using. The honey-soy baste can be kept in the refrigerator for an almost indefinite time.

To freeze: The rice and waterchestnut stuffing can be frozen. Defrost completely before using.

GILDED GAME HENS [serves 8]

Kindled by a fanciful gastronomic dream—then created for sophisticated palates and robust appetites.

8 Cornish game hens
1 onion, cut in eighths
salt and pepper
2 carrots, finely chopped
1 onion, finely chopped
2 celery stalks, finely chopped
½ cup melted butter
1 cup dry white wine
8 small slices of *Pâté Pangloss*
 (see recipe on p. 4)

3½ pounds puff pastry
 (see recipe on p. 152 or
 buy it from your favorite
 bakery—or try to find
 some frozen at your
 market)
1 egg beaten with
 2 tablespoons cold water
 (for egg wash)

For mushroom sauce:

¾ pound fresh mushrooms,
 sliced
½ cup dry white wine
1½ cups rich chicken
 stock

2 tablespoons cornstarch
 dissolved in ¼ cup cold
 water
¼ cup dry sherry
salt and pepper if needed

Season hens inside and out with salt and pepper. Place an eighth of an onion inside each and skewer closed. Tie hens so they will keep their shape. Place chopped vegetables on the bottom of a very large, shallow roasting pan, then place hens on top. Spoon melted butter over them. Roast in a 425° oven for 15 minutes, reduce temperature to 375°, add the 1 cup dry white wine and roast an additional 45 minutes or longer, basting occasionally. Hens should be nicely

58

browned and tender. Remove from oven and cool. Remove skewers and cord, then chill in the refrigerator for about 45 minutes to 2 hours—depending on your schedule.

Make the sauce: Reduce liquid in the roasting pan until dry, then remove fat from pan (use for sautéing mushrooms). Add the ½ cup wine and chicken stock to pan, scraping to deglaze—then transfer all to a saucepan. Sauté mushrooms briefly and add to sauce. Bring sauce to a boil and thicken to desired consistency with dissolved cornstarch. Season to taste. Add sherry. Set aside to be reheated before serving.

To gild the hens: Divide puff pastry into two portions. Roll each into a large square (about 18″ by 18″). Divide each large square into 4 squares (thereby making a total of 8). Place a slice of pâté on each, then top with a game hen, breast side down. Wrap carefully and seal overlaps with the prepared egg wash. Trim off any excess pastry and use it to cut out leaves for trimming. Brush outside of hens with egg wash. Trim with leaves or circles or whatever you like and brush again with egg wash. Place pastry-wrapped hens on two greased baking pans (with sides) and chill for at least 1 hour (can be as long as 4 or 5).

To bake and serve: An hour before serving preheat two ovens to 400°. (You cannot use more than one level per oven or the timing and browning won't be right. If you have only one oven plan to serve these to no more guests than you can fit game hens on one level —probably six would be maximum.) Place chilled pastry-wrapped hens in the ovens and bake for 35 to 40 minutes. If pastry tops get too brown, cover tops of hens loosely with foil. (While hens are baking, gently reheat the sauce.) Serve at once and pass the sauce separately.

Note: Don't try filling the dinner plates with other items. Serve these all alone—or perhaps with a bouquet of watercress. Follow with a green salad—then dessert if you can still find room for it.

To prepare ahead of time: The puff pastry and the pâté can both be done several days ahead and kept refrigerated. (Or—if it all seems too much—both these items can be purchased. Buy the best pâté you can find. Many bakeries will sell you puff pastry dough by the pound but it should be ordered in advance.) The game hens must be started fairly early in the day so that there is sufficient time for the two chilling periods.

To freeze: Puff pastry freezes well—a marvelous item to have on hand if you are willing to make it.

TURKEY WITH A VENERABLE CORNBREAD STUFFING [serves 8 to 10]

Cornbread Stuffing:

4 onions, finely chopped	4 cups crumbled cornbread
½ cup butter	(see recipe on p. 134)
2 cups finely chopped	3 cups bread crumbs
celery	2 or 3 teaspoons poultry
1 pound pork sausage	seasoning
salt and pepper	1 egg

Sauté onions in butter until lightly browned and tender. Add celery and cook a little longer. Remove from skillet and now brown the pork sausage. Combine all remaining ingredients and mix very thoroughly. Set aside until ready to use. (Enough for a turkey plus an extra casserole.)

Turkey:

one 10 to 12 pound turkey	½ cup melted butter or
salt and pepper	oil

Season turkey inside and out with salt and pepper. Place in a shallow roasting pan and stuff with cornbread stuffing. Skewer opening. Pour butter over the turkey and place in a 325° oven. Roast for about 3½ hours, basting about every half hour. (If turkey and stuffing are cold it will take longer.)

To prepare ahead of time: The cornbread stuffing can be readied the day before and refrigerated. Bring to room temperature before using.

To freeze: The cornbread stuffing can be frozen. Defrost overnight in the refrigerator and bring to room temperature before using.

TURKEY-MUSHROOM-HURRY-CURRY [serves 12]

2 large onions, finely
   chopped
¾ cup butter
2½ pounds fresh mush-
   rooms, sliced
juice of half a lemon
salt and pepper to taste

4 cups thickened rich turkey
   gravy (or lacking this,
   thicken some bouillon
   or other stock)
3 teaspoons or more of
   curry powder
6 or 7 cups diced cooked turkey

Sauté onions in butter until tender and lightly browned. Add mushrooms and cook another few minutes. Add lemon juice, salt and pepper, stir, cover and cook one minute. Add remaining ingredients, stir, and simmer uncovered for about 5 minutes. Taste for seasoning. Serve with white rice and with some or all of the following condiments:

sliced bananas
chopped green onions
chopped green pepper
toasted coconut
plumped raisins

chutney
crisp bacon crumbled
chopped candied ginger
chopped toasted almonds
chopped hard-cooked egg

To prepare ahead of time: The turkey curry can be prepared the day before and refrigerated. Reheat gently before serving. The condiments can be done the day before too.

To freeze: This curry can be frozen. Defrost completely, then reheat gently and serve as directed above.

Meat

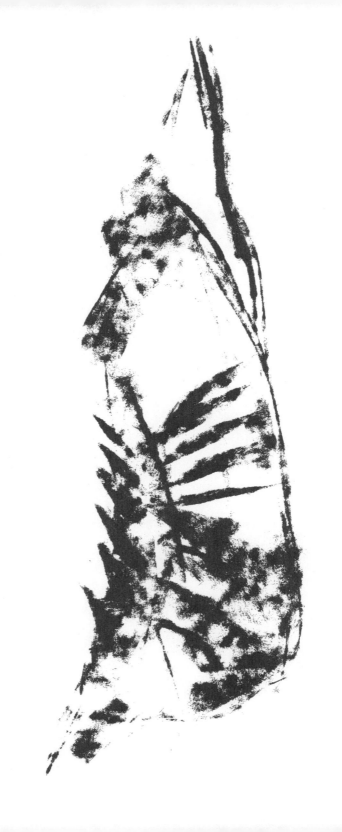

Meat

WALTER HORN'S STUFFED VEAL BREAST [serves 6 to 8]

This merits every moment you devote to its production
—superb!

one veal breast (about 6 or
   7 pounds) with a pocket
   cut for stuffing
1 onion, chopped
1 large carrot, chopped
2 celery stalks, chopped

¼ cup melted butter
salt and pepper
veal or chicken stock
Liver stuffing
   (see below)

Liver stuffing:

3 cups soaked bread (use stale
   French bread, soak in
   cold water, drain and
   squeeze to remove excess
   moisture—then measure)
½ pound liver, finely
   chopped
½ cup butter or margarine,
   softened

3 or 4 tablespoons chopped
   parsley
3 eggs, lightly beaten
salt and pepper to taste
¼ large onion, finely chopped
¼ to ½ cup finely chopped
   celery
pinch of thyme
½ teaspoon nutmeg

Combine and mix these ingredients together thoroughly.

To stuff and roast veal: Season veal lightly with salt and pepper—
inside pocket as well. (*Note:* If preferred, the veal can be blanched
with boiling water first. If so, drain and dry thoroughly.) Fill pocket
with the liver stuffing and skewer opening closed. Place the veal in a
large roasting pan on top of the finely chopped onion, carrot, and
celery. Pour the ¼ cup melted butter over the roast. Place uncovered in a 450° oven for 10 minutes, then reduce temperature to 350°.
Baste frequently until veal is a golden brown. (Stock will be needed
for this—add some to the roasting pan and keep it replenished so the

veal doesn't dry out.) Cover veal with foil and every 20 minutes or so, baste and recover. Roasting time in all should take from 2 to 3 hours depending upon: size of roast (and shape), temperature of the meat when it is placed in the oven, and your own personal taste.

To serve: Serve each guest a slice of the veal with some of the liver stuffing, topped with a little of the natural sauce that is provided from the roasting pan.

To prepare ahead of time: The stuffing can be prepared in the morning.

Note: Just as good cold the next day if you are lucky enough to have any left.

LOIN OF VEAL FALSTAFF [serves about 10]

whole loin of veal, boned
(6 to 7 pounds) as
directed below
salt and pepper
Special stuffing (see below)
2 carrots, finely chopped
1 onion, finely chopped
2 celery stalks, finely
chopped
1 bay leaf, crumbled

½ teaspoon thyme
½ cup melted butter
¼ cup sherry
3 cups stock (can be made
from veal bones)
½ cup sherry
3 tablespoons cornstarch
dissolved in ½ cup
cold water
1 tablespoon chopped parsley

Special stuffing:

1 onion, finely chopped
3 ounces ham, finely chopped
½ cup pimento-stuffed green
olives, finely chopped
2 tablespoons capers, chopped
1 pound fresh mushrooms,
finely chopped, or
ground in meat grinder

3 tablespoons butter
salt and pepper to taste
¼ teaspoon thyme
2 tablespoons chopped parsley
2 tablespoons brandy
2 egg yolks

Sauté chopped onion in the butter, then add mushrooms and cook until almost dry. Add remaining ingredients except egg yolks and simmer for 2 to 3 minutes. Remove from heat and whisk in the egg yolks. Chill.

66

To assemble and roast loin of veal: Ask your butcher to bone the loin of veal with the flank part pounded and stretched so when it is rolled it will cover everything. Season it with salt and pepper. Place stuffing between the tenderloin and sirloin and then roll up and tie. Place chopped carrots, onion, and celery in the bottom of a roasting pan along with the crumbled bay leaf and thyme. Place rolled loin on top and pour over the ½ cup of butter. Roast in a 325° oven for half an hour, add the ¼ cup sherry and continue to cook for about another hour and a half, basting frequently. (If meat is cold it will take a little longer. The veal should be cooked through but not overcooked.) Remove from oven and make the sauce.

To make the sauce and serve: Remove roast to a warm serving platter. Add the 3 cups of stock and the ½ cup sherry to the roasting pan and bring to a boil. Strain (or not as you like) into a saucepan. Thicken to your taste with the dissolved cornstarch. Add chopped parsley. Carve roast at the table and serve some of the sauce on each portion.

To prepare ahead of time: The special stuffing can be made the day before.

OSSO BUCO WITH FRESH PEAS [serves about 6]

As I remembered it from the Restaurant Aurora in Parma.

12 2-inch pieces of veal shanks	2 tablespoons tomato paste
flour	1 garlic clove, mashed
⅓ cup oil	2 cups canned tomatoes, mashed
2 onions, chopped	salt and pepper
1 large carrot, chopped	grated rind of a lemon
1 stalk celery, chopped	2 or 3 cups fresh peas
1½ cups dry white wine	

Roll veal shanks in flour and brown in the oil. Remove and place in a heavy casserole. Brown the onions, carrots, and celery in the remaining oil and add the wine, tomato paste, garlic, tomatoes, salt and pepper. Stir and bring to a boil. Pour over the veal shanks and cover casserole tightly. Place in a 300° oven and cook for one hour. Add lemon rind, reduce heat to 275° and continue cooking for about another hour or just until veal is barely tender. Add fresh peas and return to oven until peas are cooked. Keep casserole covered at all times. Serve with freshly cooked noodles or rice.

To prepare ahead of time: This can be done the day before except for the peas. Add peas at the time you plan to reheat the casserole.

To freeze: Yes, it freezes, but do so without the peas. Defrost completely, add peas, then place in oven and cook until veal is hot and peas are cooked.

LEG OF VEAL DARIUS [serves 10]

one 6 or 7 pound leg of veal, boned	1 small onion, finely chopped
salt and pepper	½ cup melted butter
	½ cup dry white wine

Season veal with salt and pepper and put into a roasting pan with the remaining ingredients. Roast uncovered at 350°—basting every 20 minutes—for about 3 hours—about 30 minutes to the pound. Serve with the natural juices. (Or if you prefer, thicken very lightly with a little cornstarch that has been dissolved in cold water.)

To prepare ahead of time: It hardly pays to try to do this ahead of time unless you are planning to serve it cold—then cook it the day before.

SIRLOIN OF VEAL SHADRACH [serves 12]

3 top sirloins of veal each weighing 2 pounds after trimming off all fat and skin (have butcher tie them so they keep a good shape)	½ cup butter
	salt and pepper
	¾ cup dry sherry
	¼ cup chopped parsley
	½ cup butter

Season veal with salt and pepper and place them in a very large shallow roasting pan. Cover with the half cup of butter. Roast at 450°

68

for 15 minutes, then at 350° for about another 45 to 60 minutes, basting every 10 or 15 minutes. Do not let meat dry out. The veal should still be a little pink—not rare and not overcooked. Remove from oven and remove strings. Place veal on a large heated platter. Add the sherry to the pan drippings and deglaze the pan. Pour into a saucepan, add remaining butter and parsley and heat but do not cook. Carve veal at the table and serve some of the sauce with the sliced portions.

A VEAL RAGOÛT [serves 6 to 8]

3 ½ to 4 pounds veal stew
 (2-inch cubes with fat
 removed)
oil or butter
½ cup flour
1 ½ cups dry white wine
1 ½ cups beef bouillon
salt and pepper
1 garlic clove, mashed
3 shallots, finely chopped

pinch of thyme
bouquet garni (bay leaf,
 celery, and parsley tied
 in a cheesecloth sack)
2 teaspoons tomato paste
24 small boiling onions,
 parboiled and drained
1 pound mushrooms,
 quartered, then sautéed
 briefly

Brown the veal in the oil or butter and place pieces as they are browned in a large casserole. Add flour to fat remaining in the pan (will need ½ cup fat to equal the flour, if not enough add more butter) and stir over low heat. Add wine and bouillon gradually, stirring constantly until mixture boils. Simmer gently while adding salt, pepper, garlic, shallots, thyme, bouquet garni, and tomato paste. Pour over veal, cover tightly and place in a 300° oven for about 1 ½ hours—or until veal is almost tender. Taste for seasoning and remove bouquet garni. Add onions and mushrooms, recover and return to oven until veal is ready. Serve with other freshly cooked vegetables such as cubed zucchini, fresh peas, carrots, green beans, etc.

To prepare ahead of time: This blanquette definitely improves if done the day before and then reheated before serving.

To freeze: Yes, this does freeze. Defrost then reheat slowly in a 300° oven.

VEAU CÔTE GRAND'MÈRE [serves 4]

I ate veal chops done in this manner in Brussels. The veal chop was marvelously cooked, then it was topped with a spray of tiny sautéed potato balls—not larger than filberts, fresh quartered mushrooms, tiny tiny very well cooked and glazed pearl onions, and tiny crisp cubes of salt pork. Beautiful and delicious! This is my adaptation.

4 perfect veal chops,
    cut 1 inch thick
salt and pepper
3 tablespoons butter
8 small mushrooms,
    quartered
2 dozen tiny pearl onions
    (don't use larger ones,
    if not in season use the
    frozen ones)
additional butter and oil for
    cooking the vegetables

½ pound salt pork, cut in
    ¼ inch dice
3 large potatoes, peeled and
    scooped into tiny balls—
    as small as possible
½ cup brown sauce (or use
    canned bouillon thickened
    slightly)
2 tablespoons Madeira
finely chopped parsley

Sauté quartered mushrooms in some butter for only a minute or two. Season lightly then place them in a small foil pan.

Cover whole unpeeled onions with water and boil for 3 minutes, then drain and peel. Season with salt, then sauté in butter until lightly browned and glazed. Place them in another foil pan.

Sauté potato balls in clarified butter or oil until tender and browned. Drain, season, and remove to another foil pan.

Place diced salt pork in a skillet with a tiny bit of oil and sauté until fat is rendered and pieces are crisp. Drain, then remove pork to another foil pan.

Shortly before serving place the 4 foil pans in a 375° oven to reheat (the potatoes will take the longest) and at about the same time, season veal chops and sauté them in the three tablespoons of butter over moderate heat until nicely browned on both sides. Add the brown sauce and the Madeira, cover skillet and simmer gently for about 5 minutes—do not overcook.

To serve: Place a cooked veal chop on a hot dinner plate and top each with a generous spoonful of the sauce. Spoon a little of each of the four items you have reheated in the oven, letting them tumble gently over the chops so that it looks like an informal spray of vegetables or flowers. Sprinkle with parsley. Serve nothing else but a light Boston lettuce salad or a plate of sliced fresh tomatoes.

To prepare ahead of time: The mushrooms, onions, salt pork, and potatoes can be prepared in the morning. Do not overcook them. Leave at room temperature covered with plastic wrap. Follow directions in above recipe for reheating.

VEAL PIPERADE   [serves about 8]

> As I prepared it one summer in Paris—equally good with fried chicken.

8 large slices of veal from the leg (or 16 small ones)	flour
	½ cup butter
	⅓ cup Vermouth
salt and pepper	*Piperade* (see below)

Piperade:

5 large green peppers, thinly sliced	2 large garlic cloves, mashed
5 medium onions, thinly sliced	4 tablespoons butter
7 small tomatoes, peeled and chopped	2 tablespoons olive oil
	salt and pepper

Sauté onions, peppers, and garlic in the butter and olive oil until tender but not brown. Stir occasionally while mixture is cooking and cook part of time covered over low heat. Season with salt and pepper. Add tomatoes and cook uncovered until some of the excess juice has cooked away and mixture is slightly thickened. Taste for seasoning. Set aside.

To prepare and serve veal: Season veal with salt and pepper and dust lightly with flour. Sauté veal in the butter over moderate heat until browned and tender. Place veal slices in a heatproof casserole as they are cooked. Add the dry Vermouth to skillet and deglaze the pan—

71

then pour this sauce over the veal. Cover veal with foil and place in a 350° oven for 5 to 10 minutes—just long enough to heat through. (While sautéeing veal, reheat piperade gently either on top of stove or in the oven.) Serve each guest some of the veal with a generous spoonful of the piperade on top or at the side.

To prepare ahead of time: The piperade can be made several days ahead and refrigerated. Reheat before serving.

To freeze: Piperade freezes. Defrost completely, then reheat gently, stirring over low heat or in a 300° oven.

FILET DE BOEUF WELLINGTON [serves about 16]

This is one of innumerable ways to accomplish this epicurean feat.

2 whole beef tenderloins (each weighing 7 pounds before trimming)
oil or clarified butter
puff pastry (need the full recipe on p. 152 or buy 3½ pounds from a good quality bakery)

Special stuffing (see below)
Madeira sauce (see below)
watercress or parsley for garnish
egg wash (1 egg beaten with 1 or 2 tablespoons of water)

Special stuffing:

2 tablespoons butter
1 clove garlic, mashed
1 small onion, finely chopped
1 pound fresh mushrooms, finely chopped or put through a meat grinder
2 teaspoons flour
1½ teaspoons salt
¼ teaspoon pepper

¼ cup cream (or milk)
4 ounces chicken liver pâté (see recipe on p. 5 or substitute finest quality you can buy)
1 tablespoon chopped parsley
3 egg yolks
1 tablespoon cognac (or brandy)

Sauté chopped onion in butter with the garlic for a few minutes. Add mushrooms, stir and cook a few more minutes. Cover and continue cooking slowly for about 2 or 3 more minutes. Sprinkle with flour, salt, pepper, and stir. Add cream (or milk) and cook and stir for a

72

minute or so. Add pâté and stir. Beat in the egg yolks and cook over very low heat, stirring constantly, for 1 or 2 minutes. Remove from heat and add parsley and cognac. Taste for seasoning. Cool, then chill. This is best made the day before. It must be absolutely cold before using.

Roasting the beef tenderloins: Trim beef of all fat, skin, and gristle. Cut off the thin tail ends (they can be used for something else, as for example, beef stroganoff). Each tenderloin will weigh about 4 pounds after trimming. Rub meat with oil or clarified butter and season well with salt and pepper. Make sure meat is at room temperature before roasting. Place in a roasting pan (or pans) and place in a 450° oven for about 10 minutes. Reduce heat to 400° and roast about 15 to 30 minutes longer, basting occasionally. Meat must be rare. You will have to judge the time yourself since the shape and temperature of the meat makes it impossible to give an exact cooking time. Remove meat from roasting pan. Cool, then chill. Best to do this in the morning of the day of your party.

Madeira sauce:

> Note: Make this sauce as soon as you have finished roasting the beef tenderloins.

1 onion, finely chopped	3 cans undiluted beef bouillon
2 carrots, finely chopped	(4½ cups)
4 tablespoons butter	⅓ cup Madeira
1 or 2 tablespoons	salt and pepper
tomato paste	¼ cup cornstarch dissolved
	in ¾ cup cold water

Sauté onions and carrots in the butter until tender and well browned. Add tomato paste and bouillon, stir, then simmer uncovered for 15 minutes. Add this and the Madeira to your roasting pan (or pans) to deglaze them by scraping all the good browned bits on inside of pans (having first, of course, removed all excess grease). Simmer two or three minutes, then strain into a saucepan. Taste for seasoning. Thicken sauce by gradually adding as much of the dissolved cornstarch as you like. Stir constantly until sauce boils. Set aside until needed. Reheat before serving.

To assemble and wrap the tenderloins: Divide puff pastry into two portions, then *for each tenderloin* follow these instructions:

1. Cover each tenderloin with stuffing—putting most of it on the top side which will be placed upside down on the pastry.

2. Roll pastry into a large rectangle, about ⅛ inch thick. Brush with egg wash.

3. Place meat on pastry with the top side down. Wrap the pastry around the meat cutting away excess pastry and place right side up on a greased baking sheet. Egg wash entire top. Decorate with pastry leaves, criss-crossing lightly with a knife. Cut a small hole in the center of top. Egg wash again. Chill until time to bake (at least one hour, but longer is fine).

Final baking: This will require either one extremely large oven or two regular size ovens. The wrapped meat cannot be crowded on to one baking pan, nor can the two be baked on two levels—timing and browning are then upset. If you have only one regular oven plan this treat for 8 guests rather than 16.

Bake wrapped tenderloins (taken directly from the refrigerator) at 400° for 40 to 50 minutes. Garnish with watercress or parsley. Slice the boeuf Wellington at table and serve some of the Madeira sauce on each portion.

To prepare ahead of time: The stuffing should be prepared the day before—or not later than early morning of your party. The tenderloins can be roasted in the morning and the Madeira sauce made. They can be wrapped in the puff pastry in the early afternoon and left in the refrigerator until just the needed time to bake.

To freeze: Puff pastry freezes so it can be made any time. So does the basic Madeira sauce—just defrost it and use as directed in the above recipe.

74

COEUR DE FILET EN FEUILLETAGE [serves 10]

A recipe generated by an extraordinary dish of the same name served to us in the restaurant of the Londonderry Hotel in London.

10 filet of beef steaks, cut
   1 ¾ inches thick, all fat
   and gristle removed
puff pastry (need the full
   recipe on p. 152 or buy
   3 ½ pounds from a
   fine bakery)
Madeira sauce (see p. 73)

salt and pepper
oil
10 small slices of *Pâté Pangloss*
   (p. 4) or some of the
   chicken liver pâté
   (p. 5)
egg wash (1 egg beaten lightly
   with 2 tablespoons water)

Season trimmed steaks generously with salt and pepper, then sauté them in oil over very high heat only until browned on both sides. Beware! They must remain very rare! Since they are wrapped in puff pastry and baked—and because they are individual portions—they will cook more in the final baking. Remove steaks from skillet, cool, then cover and chill in the refrigerator for half an hour or a little longer.

Divide puff pastry into two portions. Roll out each as thinly as possible (about ⅛ inch thick) and cut into 6 squares (thus making a total of 12). Set aside two of the squares to use later for making decorations. On the remaining 10 place a slice of *Pâté Pangloss* or a small portion of the *chicken liver pâté*. Top each with a steak. Fold pastry around each steak, sealing carefully by brushing overlapping pastry first with some of the egg wash. Place with sealed sides down on lightly greased baking pans. Make a small steam hole in the center top of each. Brush entire surface with egg wash and decorate as desired with leaves, etc. made from the pastry you set aside. Brush again with egg wash and chill in the refrigerator for 1 to 3 hours.

Place pastry-wrapped steaks in a 425° oven for 5 minutes, reduce heat to 400° and bake for about an additional 25 minutes—or until well browned. Serve at once and pass the Madeira sauce that you have previously prepared and heated.

Note: These are rather tremendous portions and should be served only to appreciative friends with healthy appetites. Accompany these glorious packages with only one additional item—especially good are fresh (not frozen) green beans.

To prepare ahead of time: The pâté, the puff pastry, and the Madeira sauce can be made several days ahead.

To freeze: Puff pastry and Madeira sauce freeze well as does the chicken liver pâté on p. 5.

STEAK AU POIVRE EN CHEMISE [serves 8]

Having eaten several variations on a theme of crêpe-embellished steak in Paris—I devised this one.

8 filet of beef steaks, cut
   1 inch thick, all fat and
   skin removed
freshly ground or cracked
   black pepper
salt
oil or clarified butter
Mushroom filling (see below)

Madeira sauce (see below)
8 large crêpes (about 10 inches
   in diameter—I use a no. 8
   iron skillet), see recipe
   on p. 8
3 teaspoons grated Parmesan
melted butter
chopped parsley

Mushroom filling:

1 pound fresh mushrooms,
   sliced
6 tablespoons finely
   chopped shallots
6 tablespoons butter

4 teaspoons flour
salt and pepper to taste
½ cup heavy cream
½ cup Madeira

Melt butter in a skillet, then add shallots and sauté gently for a few minutes. Add mushrooms and sauté for about 2 minutes. Sprinkle with flour, stir, then add cream and keep stirring until mixture begins to bubble. Reduce heat and add salt and pepper to taste. Add Madeira and gently simmer for 2 minutes. Remove from heat. Taste again for seasoning.

76

Madeira sauce:

1 large carrot, chopped	2 teaspoons tomato paste
1 onion, chopped	2 tablespoons cornstarch
1 tablespoon butter	diluted in ½ cup
2 cans undiluted bouillon	cold water
(or 3 cups of home-	¼ cup Madeira
made rich beef stock)	salt and pepper if needed

Sauté chopped carrot and onion in butter very slowly until tender and lightly browned. Add bouillon and tomato paste and simmer gently, covered, for about 15 minutes. Taste for seasoning. Thicken to taste with the dissolved cornstarch. Strain. Add Madeira, then use as needed.

To cook and assemble steaks: Have crêpes ready. If they have been made ahead and refrigerated or frozen, make certain that they are at room temperature. Warm slightly in a low oven (well wrapped in foil) only long enough to soften them so they will bend without cracking.

Season steaks by pressing pepper into both sides of the filets (amount depends on your taste)—using your hands for this task. Sprinkle with salt. Sauté steaks quickly in a heavy skillet in the oil or clarified butter. Cook only until well browned but still rare. Remove from skillet and set aside.

Place about ⅛ of the mushroom filling on each crêpe. Top with a steak, then wrap crêpes around the meat (just like you were wrapping a package). Place them seam sides down in two buttered shallow casseroles. Don't crowd them. Brush tops with melted butter and sprinkle each with about ½ teaspoon of the grated Parmesan.

Just before serving place the casseroles on the top level of your oven (or ovens) at a temperature of 450° and bake only long enough to heat—8 to 15 minutes. This will depend on the thickness of your steaks and their temperature when you place them in the oven. Meat should be hot but still rare. Garnish each with a little chopped parsley. Serve at table with the Madeira sauce. Excellent with cucumber salad—and for very hungry guests, add French fried potato baskets filled with fresh peas (see p. 100).

To prepare ahead of time: The *Mushroom filling* and the *Madeira sauce* and the crêpes can be made the day before. Be sure the mushroom mixture is at room temperature before using. And what is especially attractive about this recipe is that the whole thing can be assembled in the early afternoon, then covered with plastic wrap and left at room temperature. Proceed with the final heating shortly before you are ready to serve.

To freeze: The *Mushroom filling*, the *Madeira sauce*, and the crêpes all freeze well. Defrost completely before using.

TIMBALE MILANAISE [serves about 4]

A far less complicated version of a dish prepared by the formidable chef at the Cordon Bleu Cooking School in Paris.

½ pound fresh mushrooms
⅓ pound cooked smoked
    tongue, cut in ¼ inch
    thick slices
½ pound baked ham, cut in
    ¼ inch thick slices
1 onion, finely chopped
¼ cup butter
salt and pepper
1 6-ounce can of tomato
    paste

1½ cups beef bouillon
2 cups cooked macaroni
    (just barely tender)
⅔ cup sliced black olives
    (best to slice your own
    from the large non-pitted
    variety)
¼ cup grated Parmesan
chopped parsley

Cut mushrooms into ¼ inch thick slices, then cut slices into "batons" or sticks. Cut tongue and ham slices also into "batons"—they would then be about ¼" by ¼" by 2".

Gently sauté chopped onion in butter, stirring often. When onions are tender (about 5 minutes), add mushrooms and cook for a minute or two. Season lightly with salt and pepper. Stir in tomato paste and beef bouillon, then add macaroni and heat gently. Add tongue, ham, and olives, stir and heat a little longer. Add Parmesan and chopped parsley. (Additional grated Parmesan can be served at table for those guests who would like more.) Serve hot accompanied by your favorite tossed green salad.

78

To prepare ahead of time: This can be made the day before in the morning. Be careful not to overcook. Reheat gently in a 300° oven.

To freeze: This can be frozen. Defrost completely, then reheat gently in a 300° oven. Be sure not to overcook—it needs to be hot but does not need further cooking.

BOEUF À LA BOURGUIGNONNE [serves 8 to 10]

As I prepared it in Paris—best cooked the day before serving.

4 pounds beef stew (weight after trimming), cut in 2-inch cubes
oil
salt and pepper
2 onions, coarsely chopped
2 large garlic cloves, mashed
3 shallots, chopped
⅓ cup butter
½ cup flour
3 cups dry red Burgundy

2 cups rich beef stock
1 teaspoon sugar
1 cup tomato sauce (8-ounce can)
½ teaspoon dried sweet basil
1½ pounds fresh mushrooms
butter for cooking mushrooms
2 dozen very small carrots (or cut larger ones into smaller pieces)
2 dozen small boiling onions

Dry beef thoroughly, then brown on all sides in hot oil, removing pieces to a large casserole as they are browned. Pour out cooking oil, then add 2 cups of the wine to the skillet and deglaze the pan. Pour this over beef in casserole.

Using the same skillet, sauté onions, garlic, and shallots in the butter until golden and tender. Stir in flour. Gradually add remaining wine, beef stock, and tomato sauce and stir constantly until sauce comes to a boil. Add salt, pepper, sugar, basil, and pour over beef. Mix sauce and beef gently (use a wooden spoon). Cover tightly and place in a 275° oven. Bake for 3 or 4 hours or until tender—but not falling apart. Remove from oven, taste for seasoning, and cool. Refrigerate overnight.

The next day remove any congealed fat from casserole. Sauté mushrooms (cut in halves if very large) in some butter for a minute or so.

Cook carrots and onions separately until barely tender and drain. Add these vegetables to the beef, stir, taste again for seasoning, then cover and place again in a 300° oven until very hot. Remember to just heat not cook it!

Serve this with very fresh peas or green beans (not frozen ones!), crunchy French bread, and a good red Burgundy.

To prepare ahead of time: As already mentioned this really should be done a day ahead. This can be done several days running—even better the third or fourth day. The trick is in the reheating, cooling, and reheating. Flavors are heightened, but meat and vegetables do not overcook if you exercise care.

To freeze: Yes, this freezes, but do so without the vegetables.

BEEF, TOMATO, AND CABBAGE BORSCHT

[serves 6 to 10]

You can march far and long on this—made this way borscht becomes more stew than soup.

4 pounds of beef pot roast (such as chuck, brisket, or lean beef ribs)	3 cups canned tomatoes
	1 cup canned tomato sauce
	½ cup lemon juice
2½ quarts water	½ cup brown sugar
3 onions, diced	1 very large firm cabbage,
salt and pepper to taste	coarsely cut or shredded

Trim off excess fat from the meat. Place meat in a large pot and cover with water. Bring to a boil, then skim off scum. Add the onions, some salt and pepper, tomatoes, and tomato sauce. Cover and cook very slowly until the beef begins to get tender but is not completely cooked. Add remaining ingredients and simmer uncovered for about another hour or longer—until meat is tender. Taste for seasoning occasionally, then adjust salt, pepper, lemon juice, and sugar. Remove meat, trim, then dice and return to soup.

Serve in large bowls with quantities of caraway rye bread and sweet butter.

To prepare ahead of time: This is even better made one or two days ahead. Refrigerate, then reheat before serving. (I find it simpler to refrigerate before trimming and dicing the beef.)

To freeze: Yes, this freezes well.

EIGHT TACOS

8 tortillas	2 tablespoons green chile salsa
oil or vegetable shortening	(comes in cans)
1 pound ground beef (lean)	shredded lettuce
⅓ cup water	black olives
½ teaspoon garlic salt	tomato wedges
½ teaspoon ground cumin	radishes
½ teaspoon dried oregano	green onions
salt and pepper to taste	hot sauce (or more chile salsa)
½ cup shredded Jack cheese	

Fry the tortillas in hot oil or vegetable shortening—folding them slightly with the aid of tongs so they will later be a shape that can hold the filling. Cook them until they are crisp, then drain on paper towels.

Combine ground beef, water, garlic salt, cumin, and oregano and simmer until meat is cooked and water has evaporated. Season with salt and pepper. Remove from heat and stir in chile salsa and Jack cheese.

When ready to serve, fill the fried tortillas and place in a 350° oven, uncovered, just until hot. Serve them with the vegetables and olives at the side. Pass your favorite kind of Mexican hot sauce separately so that guests can help themselves.

To prepare ahead of time: The tortillas can be fried the day before or in the morning. Crisp them in the oven before using. The beef mixture can be prepared in the morning. Cover and leave at room temperature.

To freeze: The taco shells can be frozen. Defrost, then reheat them in the oven to make sure they are crisp.

CHILI CON CARNE MY WAY [serves 4]

2 large cloves of garlic,
  mashed
1 onion, finely chopped
1 green pepper, finely
  chopped
3 tablespoons oil
1 pound lean ground beef
1½ teaspoons salt
  (or to taste)

2 teaspoons chili powder
  [Spice Islands], or more
  if you like it hot
1 teaspoon ground cumin
½ bay leaf, crushed
3½ cups canned tomatoes
  (well mashed)
1½ cups cooked kidney beans
  (canned are fine, but be
  sure to drain them
  thoroughly)

Sauté garlic and onion in the oil until lightly browned. Add green pepper and sauté another minute. Add beef and brown, stirring, for several minutes. Add all remaining ingredients except the kidney beans. Cover and simmer over low heat for 1½ hours, stirring occasionally. Uncover, add beans and simmer an additional 1½ hours or so, again stirring occasionally.

To prepare ahead of time: This can be made one or two days ahead.

To freeze: Yes, this freezes beautifully. If so, why not double or triple the recipe.

FRENCH HOT DOGS!!

long baguette-type French
  bread
spicy frankfurters (Kosher
  type is probably the best
  here in USA)

grated imported Swiss cheese
  (or a good Cheddar)
Dijon style mustard

Cut bread into pieces about 6 or 7 inches in length, then split them in half horizontally. Heat for about 3 minutes in a 350° oven. Remove from oven and fill with the frankfurters (previously cooked in simmering water) and some of the grated cheese. Return sandwiches to the oven just long enough to heat and crisp the bread (about 3 to 5 minutes). Serve at once with mustard on the side.

82

CROWN OF LAMB [serves 6 to 8]

1 crown of lamb with about 18 to 24 rib chops	2 tablespoons cornstarch dissolved in ¼ cup cold water
salt and pepper	
1 onion	¼ cup sherry
1 ½ cups beef bouillon	paper frills for bone ends

Bring meat to room temperature. Season roast with salt and pepper. Place in a roasting pan with an onion in the center. Roast at 350° for about 1 hour and 15 minutes or to your taste. Place lamb on a large platter. Discard onion and excess fat, then add bouillon to roasting pan and bring to a boil, scraping in all the good brown parts on pan. Thicken to taste with the dissolved cornstarch. Taste for seasoning and add sherry. Place frills on bone tips.

Carve at table and serve with the sauce—excellent with a wild rice casserole (about half the amount in the recipe on p. 107 should be enough).

BUTTERFLIED LAMB CHOPS WITH ROSEMARY AND GARLIC [serves 4]

In the style of the excellent lamb chops served at The Garden restaurant in London.

4 thick French-cut lamb chops, butterflied (cut through almost to the bone, then opened and flattened like a butterfly)	3 tablespoons oil
	salt and pepper
	1 or 2 garlic cloves, mashed
	dried rosemary (about ¼ to ½ teaspoon per chop)
2 tablespoons butter	

Season chops with salt and pepper. Crush rosemary and press down into chops. Heat oil and butter, add garlic, then sauté chops quickly on both sides—they should remain pink inside. Serve at once.

LEG OF LAMB AVENUE WAGRAM [serves about 6]

1 leg of lamb
salt and pepper
2 garlic cloves, mashed
1 teaspoon salt
2 teaspoons dried rosemary
½ cup Dijon mustard
1 tablespoon water
½ cup olive oil

1 large carrot, finely chopped
2 small onions, finely chopped
1 cup dry red wine
1 cup beef stock
2 tablespoons melted butter
2 tablespoons flour
2 fresh tomatoes, coarsely
    chopped

Remove every bit of fat and skin from the outside of the lamb leg. Season lamb lightly with salt and pepper. In a small bowl mix together the garlic, 1 teaspoon salt, rosemary, mustard, and water. Beat the olive oil into this with a fork or spoon or whisk. Using this mixture completely coat the leg of lamb.

Place the chopped carrot and onions in a roasting pan and put the coated lamb on top. Roast in a 350° oven—uncovered and without basting—for 1½ to 2 hours (depending on weight of meat and how you like it cooked). Remove lamb from roasting pan. Skim off any excess fat, then add the wine and stock to pan and simmer gently. Combine butter and flour, then use it to thicken the sauce, adding it gradually and stirring constantly until sauce begins to boil. Reduce heat and simmer 2 or 3 minutes. Pour into a saucepan, add chopped tomatoes and heat for about 1 minute.

To serve: Place leg of lamb on a platter or in a shallow casserole. Pour sauce over lamb and carve, serving sauce with each portion.

To prepare ahead of time: Lamb can be cooked in the morning but roast it a shorter time. Leave at room temperature. About 30 minutes before time to serve, place leg of lamb in a 375° oven and heat—and at the same time reheat the sauce.

LAMB SHANKS BRAISED IN RED WINE   [4 servings]

4 lamb shanks, trimmed of
   all fat
salt and pepper
flour
2 tablespoons oil

1 onion, finely chopped
1 garlic clove, mashed
¾ cup dry red wine
1 cup tomato juice
pinch of oregano

Season lamb shanks with salt and pepper, roll in flour, then sauté in the oil until well browned on all sides. Add onion and garlic and cook 3 or 4 minutes, stirring to prevent burning. Add remaining ingredients, cover, and simmer over lowest heat for 1½ hours or longer—until tender. Taste for seasoning and serve with whipped potatoes.

To prepare ahead of time: These can be cooked one or two days ahead. Reheat gently either on top of stove or in the oven.

To freeze: Yes, the lamb shanks freeze. Defrost, then reheat gently.

JO ANNE COTSEN'S MAGNIFICENT MANDARIN PORK TENDERLOINS   [Serves about 12]

6 pounds of pork tenderloins
1 cup apple juice
¾ cup soy sauce
½ cup honey
2 garlic cloves, crushed
2 tablespoons grated
   fresh ginger
1 tablespoon dry mustard

2 dashes Worcestershire
½ cup brandy
10 to 12 ounces of apple or
   quince jelly
grated rind of one orange
juice of one lemon
nutmeg
halved orange slices

Place meat in a large pan (glass, enamel, or stainless steel). Combine apple juice, ½ cup of the soy sauce, honey, garlic, ginger, mustard, Worcestershire, and brandy. Pour over meat and marinate at room temperature for several hours, turning once or twice. (Or cover and marinate overnight in the refrigerator.)

Place pork in a very large roasting pan. Drain marinade into a saucepan and add the apple jelly, grated orange peel, lemon juice, and remaining ¼ cup of soy sauce. Heat and stir until jelly has melted.

Pour some of this mixture over the pork and place meat in a 350° oven. Bake for 1¼ to 1½ hours, basting occasionally and adding additional marinade as needed. Remove from oven and sprinkle meat with a little nutmeg. Slice and garnish with halved orange slices. Serve with the sauce and with steamed rice.

To prepare ahead of time: Jo Anne says that this can be "held" for an indefinite dinner hour since it is hard to overcook. Keep meat warm in a very low oven.

MARY CULLINS' NEW YEARS EVE BARBECUED PIG'S FEET   [serves 4 to 6]

6 pig's feet, split
boiling water
2 garlic cloves, whole
2 small, hot red peppers
2 teaspoons salt

1½ cups hickory smoked barbecue sauce (either buy a bottled variety or make your own)

Place pig's feet in a large roasting pan and cover with boiling water. Add garlic, peppers, and salt. Cover, then place in a 400° oven for 20 minutes. Reduce heat to 350° and cook for about 2 hours. Turn pig's feet and return to oven for another 45 minutes, or until tender. Add barbecue sauce, spooning it over the pig's feet, cover and return to oven for 30 to 45 minutes. Remove cover and cook about 15 to 20 minutes longer. Serve with black-eyed peas (see recipe on p. 103).

To prepare ahead of time: These can be cooked the day before. Reheat in the oven.

To freeze: Yes, these can be frozen. Defrost, then reheat in the oven.

EILEEN TAYLOR'S SPECIAL PORK CHOPS   [serves 6]

These are foolproof, effortless, and delectable!

6 lean and very thick pork chops (ask your butcher to cut them 1½ inches thick)

½ cup apple sauce
2 tablespoons ketchup
2 tablespoons soy sauce
grated rind of 1 lemon

Combine apple sauce, ketchup, soy sauce, and grated lemon rind. Place pork chops in an ovenproof casserole and salt them lightly. Cover with the sauce. Bake at 350° for about 1 hour.

A LOAF OF HAM   [serves about 6]

1 ¼ pounds baked ham   1 teaspoon dry mustard
1 small onion   ¼ teaspoon oregano
½ green pepper   ¼ cup chili sauce
1 cup dry bread crumbs   ¼ teaspoon pepper
¾ cup milk   salt only if needed
2 eggs

Put the ham, onion, and green pepper through the meat grinder. Combine thoroughly with remaining ingredients. Grease a loaf pan and fill with the mixture. Bake at 450° for 10 minutes, then at 350° for about 30 minutes longer.

To prepare ahead of time: The ham loaf mixture can be combined in the morning, then bake before serving. This is excellent served cold the next day.

GARBURE   [serves 6 to 10]

I first ate Garbure—a Basque soup—at St-Jean-Pied-de-Port in Paris; this version, planned as a substantial main course, is thicker and meatier.

1 cup dried lima beans, soaked   4 celery stalks, sliced
    overnight in 3 cups water   ½ large cabbage, coarsely
3 pound piece of smoked ham   sliced or shredded
3 boiling potatoes, cubed   ¼ teaspoon thyme
4 quarts water   ½ teaspoon basil
1 garlic clove, mashed   ½ teaspoon oregano
2 onions, chopped   salt and pepper to taste
4 carrots, sliced

Combine soaked lima beans with the ham, potatoes, 4 quarts of water, garlic, onions, and carrots. Bring to a boil. Add remaining ingredients, cover and simmer for about 2 hours. Remove cover and continue to simmer for about another hour or so. Taste occasionally for seasoning. Remove ham, dice meat, then return to soup.

To prepare ahead of time: This can be made a day ahead and refrigerated—even better the second and third day.

To freeze: This freezes well.

Vegetables and Starches

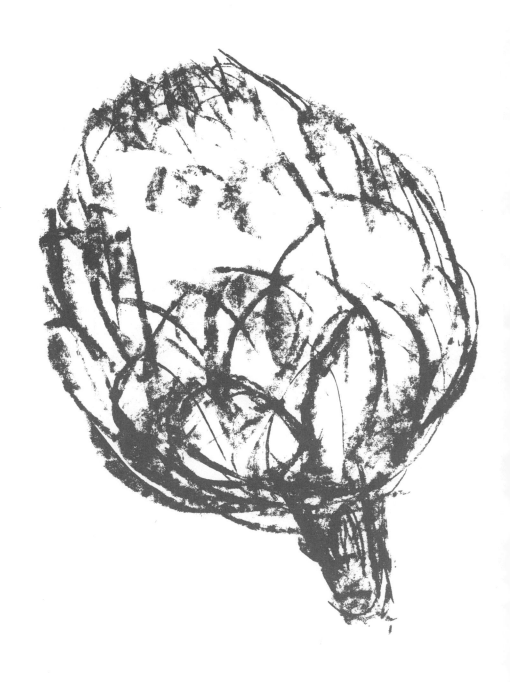

Vegetables and Starches

JO ANNE COTSEN'S VERY SPECIAL ARTICHOKES
[Serves 4]

Jo Anne says these are delicious and messy—no problem
—just provide extra paper napkins.

4 large artichokes	1 tablespoon dried thyme
4 garlic cloves	¼ cup chopped parsley
¾ cup olive oil	melted butter flavored
1 tablespoon dried oregano	with garlic

Thoroughly soak artichokes. Cut tops off about ¼ to ⅓ of the way
down from the top. Trim bottoms. Put 1 large peeled garlic clove
deep into each center. Place artichokes in a large pot and cover the
bottom with about 1 inch of water and add a little salt. Dribble olive
oil over the tops. Divide and sprinkle the oregano and thyme over the
tops of the artichokes, then cover tightly and bring to a boil. As soon
as water boils, reduce heat and simmer over low heat for 1 to 1½
hours depending on size of artichokes. About ½ hour before artichokes are done sprinkle with the parsley. Serve hot with garlic
flavored butter.

To prepare ahead of time: **Undercook** somewhat, then turn up heat
and finish cooking about ½ hour before serving. No need to worry
since as Jo Anne points out, artichokes are one of the few vegetables
that are good when extremely well cooked.

ARTICHOKES STUFFED WITH FRESH GREEN
BEANS
[serves 20]

A lot of work but splendid for a buffet dinner—

20 large fresh artichokes	salt and pepper
3 lemons	melted butter
2¼ pounds fresh green beans	

Trim artichokes of all outside tough leaves, then cut off ⅔ of each artichoke from the top. Trim and smooth places where the tough leaves have been removed. (One must be ruthless about removing the outside leaves and about discarding the top ⅔ of the artichoke!) Cook the artichokes in a huge pot of salted boiling water to which you have added the juice of 3 lemons. As soon as they are tender drain them carefully and place upside down on a rack to cool. Then carefully with the aid of a teaspoon, remove the inside choke of each.

Prepare green beans by cutting them French style (julienne) and then cutting them crosswise into 1-inch pieces. Cook in a large quantity of boiling water, uncovered, until just tender. Don't overcook. Drain thoroughly, then season with salt, pepper, and a generous amount of melted butter.

To assemble and serve: Place artichokes in one or two greased shallow casseroles. Season lightly with salt and pepper. Brush or sprinkle with melted butter. Fill the hollows with the previously prepared green beans. Cover lightly with foil and place in a 350° oven until very hot—but do not overcook. Place these on a large heated platter and serve.

To prepare ahead of time: The artichokes and the green beans can be cooked the day before. Keep covered and refrigerated. Bring to room temperature before heating—fill artichokes, then proceed as directed above.

To freeze: I am prejudiced against frozen vegetables—so—don't freeze these. If you go to this much trouble they should be served at their very best.

ASPARAGUS, CHINESE STYLE [serves 10]

5 pounds fresh asparagus
2 to 4 tablespoons oil
    (peanut or vegetable)
1 garlic clove, mashed

1-inch piece of fresh ginger,
    peeled and finely chopped
salt
a very little pepper

Break off or cut off the tough ends of asparagus. Peel the outer part of asparagus toward the ends using a potato peeler. Slice asparagus on a sharp diagonal in about ¾ inch slices.

Heat oil in a very large skillet or in a large cooking pot. Add garlic and ginger, then add asparagus and toss with two spoons and fry over high heat for about 1 minute. Season, then continue tossing and frying over high heat for 1 or 2 more minutes. Remove from heat and serve at once.

To prepare ahead of time: The cleaning and slicing of the asparagus can be done in the morning. Keep refrigerated in a large plastic bag.

HOT FRESH ASPARAGUS VINAIGRETTE [serves 4]

2 pounds fresh asparagus
¾ cup French dressing
  (see recipe on p. 112)

salt and pepper if needed

Snap or cut off tough ends of asparagus. Peel bottom part of asparagus with potato peeler. Bring a large pot of water to boiling, then add asparagus and some salt. Cook rapidly, uncovered, only until crisp tender. Drain and place hot asparagus in a very hot serving dish. Spoon French dressing over asparagus and serve as soon as possible.

BROCCOLI EN CHEMISE [serves 8]

1 large bunch of broccoli
  (or 2 small)
salt and pepper
melted butter

24 crêpes, 6 or 7 inches in diameter (need about double the recipe on p. 9)

Trim broccoli and cook just until barely tender. Drain, then trim again separating the upper parts from the heavier stalks. (Set aside the latter for family use another time in something like cold broccoli vinaigrette or for a broccoli soup.) Season with salt, pepper, and melted butter.

Fold crêpes in quarters, then tuck in some of the broccoli flowerettes. Place filled crêpes in a large shallow buttered casserole. Brush well

93

with melted butter. Cover lightly with foil. Place in a 350° oven only long enough to heat. Serve with Hollandaise or Béarnaise sauce—or —with melted butter.

To prepare ahead of time: This can be assembled in the morning. Cover and leave at room temperature. Shortly before serving proceed with the final heating.

To freeze: Crêpes can be frozen. Defrost completely, then while still in their foil wrapping place in a low oven only long enough to make them soft enough to fold without cracking.

FRESH CARROTS WITH GREEN ONIONS [serves 6]

3 cups thinly sliced carrots
¼ cup butter

6 to 8 green onions, chopped
salt and pepper to taste

Place carrots with butter in a skillet over high heat. Cover and cook for ½ minute. Stir and reduce heat to lowest possible temperature, cover and cook only until just barely tender. Season. Add green onions, then cook over moderate heat for about 1 minute.

To prepare ahead of time: These can be cooked in the morning. Do not overcook. Reheat over low heat, stirring occasionally, just before serving.

CARROTS WITH GREEN PEPPER [serves 6 to 8]

10 fresh carrots
3 green peppers

⅓ cup melted butter
salt and pepper

Clean carrots, then cut them into sticks about ¼ inch thick and about 3 inches long. Clean green peppers and cut them into strips, roughly the same size as the carrots. Place these in alternating layers with salt, pepper, and butter in between in a casserole with a tight-fitting cover. Bake at 350° for about 1½ hours or until carrots are tender.

To prepare ahead of time: This can be done the day before—be sure not to overcook. Refrigerate, then bring to room temperature several hours before serving. Reheat in a 350° oven only until hot.

CELERY, GREEN PEPPER, AND GREEN ONIONS

[serves 4 to 6]

3 cups thinly sliced celery
¼ cup butter
1 green pepper, coarsely
   chopped

4 green onions, chopped
salt and pepper to taste

Place butter in a large skillet or pot. Add celery and cook over high heat, stirring, for about 1 minute. Add chopped green pepper and cover, then cook for about 2 minutes. Add green onions, salt and pepper, and cover again and cook 1 minute. Serve at once.

Note: The vegetables should still have a pleasant crisp texture.

To prepare ahead of time: Chopping and slicing of vegetables can be done in the morning.

FRIED CORN

[serves 4 to 6]

6 large ears of fresh corn
½ cup butter
½ teaspoon sugar

salt and pepper to taste
½ cup heavy cream

Scrape ears of corn by slitting kernels with a sharp knife, then scraping downwards, thus extracting the inside part of the corn kernels. Or if you have a gadget called a corn scraper, use that.

Heat butter in a heavy skillet, then add corn and sauté over moderate heat, stirring constantly, for several minutes. Reduce heat, add remaining ingredients and stir until mixture begins to simmer. Cook, stirring occasionally, until mixture thickens, about 10 to 15 minutes. Taste for seasoning and serve very hot.

To prepare ahead of time: This can be made the day before or in the morning. Reheat gently, stirring often to prevent sticking.

MUSHROOM MELODY [serves 4 to 6]

1 pound fresh mushrooms
juice of ½ lemon
¼ cup butter
salt and pepper to taste
1 tablespoon flour

1 teaspoon onion powder
1 cup sour cream
3 green onions, chopped
2 teaspoons chopped parsley

Clean and dry mushrooms. Slice them thickly. Sauté in the butter for about half a minute, then add the lemon juice, salt, pepper, flour, and onion powder. Stir. Remove from heat and stir in the sour cream. Return to heat and cook, stirring constantly, until mixture has thickened. Remove from heat and spoon into a serving casserole. Top with chopped green onions and parsley and place in a 350° oven for 5 to 7 minutes. Serve hot with almost anything: roast beef, steak, hamburgers, fried chicken, and—well, you name it!

To prepare ahead of time: This can be made in the morning or the day before. Refrigerate, then shortly before serving (an hour or two) bring to room temperature and proceed with the final heating.

To freeze: Yes, this can be frozen. Defrost and bring to room temperature, then proceed with the final heating.

CHAMPIGNONS FANTASTIQUES [serves 10 to 16]

This was created out of my need to do mushrooms easily, deliciously, and for very many people.

2 to 4 dozen giant fresh
    mushrooms

1 cup melted butter (or more)
salt and pepper

Clean mushrooms and dry thoroughly with paper towels. Dip each mushroom in melted butter, then place in a baking-serving dish and season with salt and pepper. Don't crowd. If necessary use more than one dish. Bake in a 400° oven for 10 to 15 minutes. The mushrooms should still be firm so don't overcook.

To prepare ahead of time: Mushrooms can be dipped in butter and arranged in their baking dish in the morning. Leave at room temperature lightly covered. Just before serving proceed with the baking as directed.

FRESH PEAS AND MUSHROOMS [serves 10]

5 pounds of fresh peas
½ pound fresh mushrooms,
   sliced

¼ cup butter (or more)
salt and pepper to taste

Cook peas uncovered in a large quantity of boiling water. After peas begin to boil cook only for 2 minutes, then drain. Sauté mushrooms in the butter for about 2 minutes and season with salt and pepper. Combine with peas, adding more butter if you like. Arrange in a heatproof dish or casserole and briefly heat, covered, in a 350° oven —only long enough to make certain that vegetables are hot.

To prepare ahead of time: This can be done in the morning. Leave at room temperature lightly covered. Reheat as directed in recipe above.

PEPPERS IN TOMATO SAUCE [serves 4]

Inspired by a something similar served to us at the Villa Scacciapensieri near Siena.

4 large green peppers
1 onion, finely chopped
1 garlic clove, mashed
3 tablespoons oil

salt and pepper to taste
¼ teaspoon sweet basil
2 cups canned tomatoes,
   well mashed

Burn skin of peppers over a gas flame or under a broiler. Place peppers in a brown paper bag to steam for 15 or 20 minutes, then peel, remove seeds, and cut in largish pieces or slices.

Make tomato sauce: Sauté onion and garlic in oil over moderate heat until tender but not brown. Add salt, pepper, sweet basil, and tomatoes. Simmer covered for about 15 minutes. Uncover and simmer another 10 or 15 minutes. Taste for seasoning. Add peppers, cover and simmer for 5 to 10 minutes.

To prepare ahead of time: This can be made the day before or in the morning but reserve final cooking until just before serving. I usually combine everything in a casserole and then heat it in a 350°

97

oven for about 15 minutes. The peppers are then only partially cooked and retain some firmness.

To freeze: The tomato sauce can be frozen. Defrost completely before using, heat, then add prepared peppers.

SPINACH IN CRÊPES   [serves 12]

These can serve as both green vegetable and starch.

24 crêpes, 6 or 7 inches in diameter (need about double the recipe on p. 9)	½ cup milk
	2 teaspoons salt
	½ teaspoon pepper
3 12-ounce packages of chopped frozen spinach	¼ teaspoon nutmeg
	½ cup grated Parmesan
¼ cup butter	additional grated Parmesan
¼ cup flour	melted butter
1 cup light cream	finely chopped parsley

Defrost spinach and drain *very thoroughly*. Melt the ¼ cup butter, stir in flour and cook over low heat for 1 minute. Remove from heat and stir in cream and milk. Return to heat and cook, stirring constantly, until mixture comes to a boil. Reduce heat and simmer slowly for a few minutes, adding salt, pepper, and nutmeg. Stir in the ½ cup of Parmesan. Add the well drained spinach and stir over low heat for about 1 minute. Taste for seasoning. Remove from heat.

Fill each crêpe with some of the spinach mixture and roll up. Place rolled crêpes seam side down in buttered shallow casseroles. Brush tops of rolls with melted butter and sprinkle lightly with grated Parmesan. Place in a 350° oven and bake only until hot (anywhere from 5 to 15 minutes). If desired you can place them briefly under a broiler unit for a minute or so to brown the tops. Remove from oven, sprinkle with chopped parsley and serve.

To prepare ahead of time: These can be assembled in the morning. Cover with plastic wrap and set aside at room temperature until time to heat. Then proceed as directed in the above recipe.

To freeze: Crêpes can be frozen. Defrost completely, then while they are still in their foil wrapping, place in a low oven only long enough to make them soft enough to roll without cracking.

BAKED CHERRY TOMATOES [serves 12 to 16]

3 baskets of cherry tomatoes   salt and pepper
⅓ cup melted butter

Make sure tomatoes are at room temperature. Remove stems. Place tomatoes in a baking dish that you can serve from. Pour melted butter over tomatoes, season with salt and pepper, toss lightly, and just before serving place in a 400° oven for about 5 minutes. These don't need to cook much—just need heating through.

POMMES MACAIRE [serves 4]

First tried these potatoes at the scenic Cap Estel Hotel
at Eze-Bord-de-Mer on the French Riviera.

4 baking potatoes   salt and pepper to taste
½ cup butter (soft)

Bake potatoes. Scoop out insides and mash them with a fork. Do not try to sieve them or whip them. Add butter, salt and pepper. Butter 4 individual shallow casseroles (or one larger one) and fill with the potatoes. Bake them uncovered in a 400° oven. They should be well browned top and bottom.

Serve these potatoes either unmolded—or—directly from their casseroles.

Note: Any number of servings can be prepared this way—just remember the proportion of 2 tablespoons of butter for each potato.

To prepare ahead of time: Potatoes can be baked in the morning and arranged in the casseroles. Cover lightly, then before serving proceed with the final baking.

GRATED POTATO MUFFINS [makes 6]

2 large baking potatoes	⅛ teaspoon baking powder
¼ teaspoon salt	2 tablespoons flour
⅛ teaspoon pepper	1 egg
1 tablespoon grated onion	

Grate potatoes. Beat remaining ingredients together, then combine with potatoes. Grease muffin tins quite heavily with vegetable shortening. Fill tins about ¾ full. Bake at 400° for about 1 hour or longer —until very brown.

To prepare ahead of time: These can be baked in the morning. Leave at room temperature, then reheat in oven before serving.

FRENCH FRIED POTATO BASKETS [makes about 10]

8 large baking potatoes	salt
oil or vegetable shortening	

You will need a special gadget for this production, namely, a French potato basket fryer—or—lacking this you can make one of your own by combining two fine metal sieves (one about 3½ inches in diameter, the other about 4½ inches in diameter). You will then need a piece of wire or some such thing to hold them together after the potatoes have been fitted in.

Plan to make one potato basket at a time. Ideal for this job is a thermostatically regulated deep fat fryer—otherwise use a deep fat thermometer. Oil or shortening should be set at 375°. Shred one potato on a Mouli Salad Maker—using the disk with holes ⅛ inch in diameter (or lacking this gadget, find a shredder with holes of similar width). Dip *both parts* of potato basket fryer (or your two sieves) in the hot oil, then line the larger part (or sieve) with shredded potatoes. Fit smaller basket on top and clamp or fasten closed. Fry in deep fat until well browned. Remove, drain, unfasten and remove basket. If potatoes stick, don't be afraid to hit it firmly on your table. (If the fryer-basket has been dipped in oil before being filled, and if the potatoes have been cooked until brown, you should not have any problem.)

Continue with the other potatoes—and—remember to dip your basket-fryer in hot oil each time before filling. When all baskets have been made sprinkle them lightly with salt. Just before serving place potato baskets on a baking sheet and reheat, uncovered, in a 400° oven. This shouldn't take long—watch that they do not burn.

To prepare ahead of time: These can be made in the morning. Leave at room temperature lightly covered. Before serving, reheat as directed above.

To freeze: These are amazingly good after freezing. Perhaps not quite as good as when made and eaten the same day. (Freeze them in plastic bags—then reheat in the oven as directed above.)

Note: Fill these delicious potato baskets with fresh peas or green beans and serve with hamburgers, steaks, or almost anything else. They also make an excellent lunch or supper filled with scrambled eggs.

PESTO FOR PASTA [enough for 6 to 8 small servings]

You must use fresh sweet basil for this dazzlingly delicious sauce. So—grow your own—then double or triple this recipe, for happily this freezes magnificently.

⅓ cup piñon nuts
1 cup sweet basil leaves (be sure to remove stems)
2 garlic cloves, mashed
1 teaspoon salt
½ teaspoon pepper
1 tablespoon very hot water

½ cup olive oil
¾ cup grated Parmesan
¾ pound very thin spaghetti (or other thin pasta)
¼ cup butter (or more)
additional grated Parmesan to be served at table

Whirl piñon nuts in a blender, then set them aside. Place sweet basil, water, and olive oil in the blender and purée. Place this in a bowl and stir in the ground piñons. Beat in the garlic, salt, pepper, and the ¾ cup grated Parmesan.

Cook the spaghetti in a large quantity of boiling, salted water until barely tender (*al dente*). Drain thoroughly and then toss with the butter. Add the prepared pesto and toss again. Serve on hot plates and pass the additional grated Parmesan for guests to help themselves.

To prepare ahead of time: The pesto sauce will keep in the refrigerator for several weeks. Make certain that it is tightly covered or in a tightly sealed jar. Bring to room temperature and stir before using.

To freeze: Yes, as already mentioned, the pesto sauce does freeze very well. Defrost completely, bring to room temperature, stir, and then use.

Note: Nice to serve as a first course for an "Italian style" feast—main course might be a favorite veal dish served with a salad of sliced tomatoes and red onions (see recipe on p. 114).

BERTA'S BLACK BEANS FROM PAT ALTMAN
[makes about 6 quarts]

3 pounds black beans (Cuban or Mexican)	2 tablespoons chopped parsley
3 bay leaves	1 teaspoon oregano
1 tablespoon baking soda	½ teaspoon ground cumin
3 large garlic cloves, mashed	½ teaspoon black pepper
4 onions	4 peeled tomatoes
½ cup olive oil	(can use canned)
2 green peppers	about 1 tablespoon salt
1 sweet red pepper	(may need more, taste!)

Carefully pick over the beans for foreign objects such as pebbles, etc. Wash and drain beans. Soak beans overnight in water to cover. Next morning add more water, bay leaves, and baking soda. Bring to a boil, skimming constantly until no foam rises. Boil slowly until beans are tender. Add salt.

Meanwhile (while beans are simmering), chop onions and sauté in the oil until golden, then add garlic, black pepper, and parsley. Chop green and red peppers and add them too. Sauté for several minutes. Pour this mixture into the cooked beans and add the chopped tomatoes, oregano, and cumin. Stir. Water should be mostly, but not completely absorbed by now. Cook approximately another half hour. Taste for seasoning. You can mash some of the beans to thicken juices if you want. Place the entire bean mixture in a very large casserole and bake uncovered in a 350° oven for about 1 hour.

Serve with onion rings and avocado slices.

To prepare ahead of time: These can be prepared several days ahead. Reheat in the oven.

To freeze: Yes, these freeze magnificently.

NOODLES BAKED WITH SOUR CREAM AND COTTAGE CHEESE
[serves 4 to 6]

3 ounces noodles
1 cup cottage cheese
1 ½ cups sour cream
salt and pepper to taste

1 green onion, finely chopped
1 teaspoon Worcestershire sauce

Cook noodles in boiling, salted water until just barely tender. Do not let them become mushy. Drain. Combine remaining ingredients and mix with the noodles. Pour into a greased casserole and bake at 350° for 30 to 40 minutes. Serve very hot. Additional sour cream can be passed separately.

To prepare ahead of time: Noodles can be cooked and drained in the morning, then combined with the other ingredients and baked in the evening. If desired, the casserole can be baked the day before or in the morning and then reheated. However—the texture is somewhat changed—for it then loses its creaminess and is more like a baked pudding.

MARY CULLINS' NEW YEARS EVE BLACK-EYED PEAS
[serves about 8]

¾ pound smoked bacon, in one piece
1 pound dried black-eyed peas
2 garlic cloves, whole

1 teaspoon salt (may need more)
1 tablespoon sugar
¾ pound chorizo sausage
5 cups boiling water

Cut bacon into largish cubes and place them in a Dutch oven. Pick over peas and discard the bad ones along with any foreign objects such as pebbles, etc. Add peas to bacon and pour 5 cups of boiling water over them. Add garlic, salt, and sugar. Cover and place in a 350° oven for about 1½ hours. Add chorizo, cut in chunks, recover and return to oven for about 45 minutes. Taste for seasoning and add more salt if needed. Remove cover and return to oven for about 45 minutes longer. Remove from oven and skim off any excess fat that remains on the surface. Serve hot along with cornbread and barbecued pigs' feet (see recipe on p. 86).

To prepare ahead of time: This can be cooked the day before. Reheat in the oven before serving.

To freeze: These freeze very well. Defrost, then reheat in the oven.

JO ANNE COTSEN'S BROWN RICE WITH PINE NUTS AND A SPICY APRICOT ACCOMPANIMENT
[Serves 8 to 10]

Brown rice:

2 cups brown rice	½ cup melted butter
4 cups water	¾ teaspoon nutmeg
1 teaspoon salt	2 teaspoons turmeric
1 cup onions, chopped	⅔ cup pine nuts, browned
1 garlic clove, minced	a little
salt and pepper	¼ cup seedless raisins or
	currants

Wash rice, then add water and salt. Let boil 2 minutes in a heavy pot, cover and simmer until water is absorbed—about 45 to 50 minutes. When rice is tender remove from heat. If it isn't dry, place in a warm oven for a few minutes.

Sauté onions and garlic in the butter until tender, then add remaining ingredients and mix thoroughly with the rice. Place in a serving casserole and reheat in a moderate oven for a few minutes.

To prepare ahead of time: This can be made the day before. Refrigerate overnight. Bring to room temperature the next day, cover with foil, then heat in a 300° oven.

To freeze: This can be frozen. Defrost and bring to room temperature. Cover with foil, then heat in a 300° oven.

Spicy Apricot Accompaniment:

1½ cups apricot purée (about 1 10-oz. package dried apricots cooked until tender in water to cover, then puréed in a blender)	1½ teaspoons curry powder 3 tablespoons honey 1 teaspoon almond extract 2 tablespoons dry mustard 1 tablespoon powdered ginger 2 or 3 tablespoons sherry

Combine and mix all the ingredients. Serve at room temperature, or if preferred, chilled.

To prepare ahead of time: This can be made several days ahead. Store in the refrigerator.

To freeze: This can be frozen. Defrost and bring to room temperature (or serve slightly chilled).

RICE AND GARBANZO CASSEROLE   [serves 6 to 8]

1 onion, finely chopped	1 8-ounce can tomato sauce
1 garlic clove, mashed	1½ cups hot beef stock
⅓ cup oil	1½ cups cooked garbanzos
1 cup uncooked rice	salt and pepper to taste

Sauté onion and garlic in the oil for about 5 minutes (over low to moderate heat). Add rice, then sauté for 2 or 3 minutes, stirring occasionally. Add remaining ingredients. Cover tightly and simmer for 25 minutes. Remove cover to dry for a minute or two when finished cooking.

To prepare ahead of time: This can be made a day ahead or in the morning. Refrigerate, then spoon into another casserole (separating rice grains with your hands), cover with foil and reheat in a 325° oven.

To freeze: This can be frozen. Defrost completely. Then cover with foil and reheat in a 325° oven.

RICE CASSEROLE WITH
PIMENTO AND PIÑON NUTS [serves 12 to 16]

8 cups cooked rice (cold)	½ cup chopped pimento
2 onions, finely chopped	¾ cup piñon nuts
½ cup butter	salt and pepper to taste

Sauté chopped onions in the butter until tender, then add piñon nuts and sauté 1 or 2 more minutes. Add pimento and rice and season to taste. Mix thoroughly. Place in a lightly greased casserole, cover with foil and place in a 325° oven until hot.

To prepare ahead of time: This can be prepared the day before or in the morning—do the final oven heating before serving.

To freeze: This can be assembled and then frozen. Defrost, then proceed with the final oven heating as directed in the recipe.

SPINACH AND RICE [serves 12 to 18]

Ideal for a buffet supper.

8 to 10 cups cooked rice (cold)	4 10-ounce packages of frozen,
2 onions, finely chopped	chopped spinach
½ cup butter	salt and pepper to taste

Sauté onions in the butter until lightly browned and tender. Cook spinach, then drain *very thoroughly*. Combine onions, spinach, and rice and season to taste. Place in a lightly greased casserole and cover with foil. Place in a 325° oven just until it is piping hot.

To prepare ahead of time: This can be assembled the day before or in the morning. Do the final heating before serving.

To freeze: This can be assembled and frozen. Defrost, then proceed with the final heating.

WILD RICE AND MUSHROOM CASSEROLE

[serves 12 to 16]

8 to 10 cups cooked wild rice
(about 3 cups of raw
rice), cold
1 small onion, finely chopped
¼ cup butter

¾ pound fresh mushrooms,
sliced
½ cup butter
salt and pepper to taste

Sauté chopped onion in the ¼ cup butter just until lightly browned. Remove from skillet. Add the ½ cup butter to the skillet and sauté the sliced mushrooms for a minute or two. Season. Mix onions and mushrooms with the wild rice and taste for seasoning. Spoon into a lightly greased casserole and cover with foil. Place in a 325° oven just until very hot.

To prepare ahead of time: This can be assembled the day before or in the morning. Do the oven heating before serving.

To freeze: This can be assembled and frozen. Defrost, then proceeed with the final oven heating.

Salads

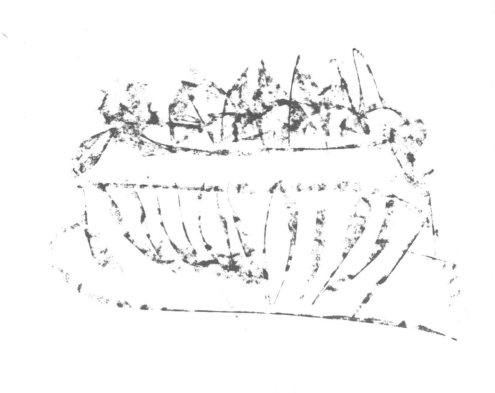

WALTER HORN'S SALAD
OF DANDELION GREENS [serves 6 to 8]

> Dandelion greens used to be gathered in the fields . . . improved varieties are now cultivated, but you may have to ask for them in specialty produce markets. These tantalizing, slightly bitter greens are well worth the search.

1 large bunch of dandelion greens
3 or more ripe tomatoes, cut in small wedges
4 green onions, chopped
French dressing (see recipe on p. 112 or use your own favorite)

Wash thoroughly, drain, and dry the greens. Cut in any desired length and place in a salad bowl. Sprinkle with the chopped green onions and scatter the tomato wedges over the salad. Add French dressing, toss and serve.

To prepare ahead of time: The salad can be completely arranged in a bowl, covered tightly with plastic wrap and refrigerated in the morning. Toss with dressing just before serving.

CRUDITÉS

> Every assortment and variation on the theme of raw vegetables—*crudités*—is served as a first course in France and why not—attractive, refreshing, and non-fattening!

raw carrots, shredded
celery, shredded or diced or sliced
green peppers, thinly sliced
tomatoes, wedges or slices
cucumbers, slices or wedges
red cabbage, coarsely shredded
chopped green onions (optional)
French dressing (see recipe on p. 112)

Arrange the vegetables on chilled individual serving plates—keeping in mind color and design. Sprinkle with chopped green onion and spoon on the French dressing. (For really serious dieters, just use some lemon juice.)

To prepare ahead of time: Plates of vegetables can be arranged several hours ahead, covered with plastic and refrigerated. Spoon on the dressing just before serving.

SALADE VERTE À MA FAÇON [serves about 12]

2 large heads of romaine
2 heads of red lettuce
1 head of curly endive
French dressing (see recipe below or use your own favorite)

6 green onions, finely chopped
fresh oregano (or some other fresh herb) finely chopped—as much as your taste dictates

Wash, dry, and chill the romaine, red lettuce, and curly endive.

French dressing:

3 teaspoons salt
½ teaspoon black pepper
⅛ teaspoon paprika
1 teaspoon dry mustard
1 or 2 garlic cloves, mashed
1 or 2 teaspoons sugar

2 teaspoon Worcestershire sauce
1 cup cider vinegar (or lemon juice if you want a lemon French dressing)
2 cups salad oil

Combine all the ingredients except the oil and beat thoroughly. Then, using a whisk or a rotary egg beater, beat in the oil. Store in tightly sealed jars in the refrigerator.

Prepare salad: Tear (or cut) greens and place in a very large salad bowl. Sprinkle with the chopped green onions and fresh herb. Add as much French dressing as you like, toss, and serve on iced salad plates.

To prepare ahead of time: The salad can be assembled in the morning and kept refrigerated—covered tightly with plastic wrap. Add French dressing just before serving.

Note: Real French dressing does not contain sugar, nor would any-think like Worcestershire be used. I use the term in its more general sense as it is applied in this country to miscellaneous kinds of flavored oil and vinegar dressings.

ENDIVE SALAD

Belgian endive (need about one per person)
a fresh herb: tarragon or oregano or sweet basil—finely chopped

a little chopped green onion (but don't overdo it)
French dressing made with lemon juice (see recipe on p. 112)

Separate endive leaves and if they are large, cut or break them crosswise. Place in a large salad bowl and sprinkle with the chopped herb (use just one kind) and the green onion. Cover completely and tightly with plastic wrap and refrigerate. Just before serving toss with the French dressing. Serve on iced salad plates.

Note: I think it best to serve this salad as a separate course, preferably after the main course. The endive is delicate and to be truly appreciated should be eaten alone.

To prepare ahead of time: The salad can be assembled in the morning and kept tightly covered and refrigerated until time to toss with the French dressing.

Special hint: To make this salad taste especially good (and other green salads as well), keep salad plates in your freezer until time to serve.

HEARTS OF BOSTON (BUTTER) LETTUCE WITH A CHOPPED EGG DRESSING   [serves 10]

10 small heads of Boston (butter) lettuce
1 cup mayonnaise
½ cup sour cream
⅓ cup chili sauce
2 tablespoons minced, pimento-stuffed green olives

2 hard-cooked eggs, chopped
1 teaspoon chopped parsley
2 green onions, finely chopped
juice of half a lemon
1 teaspoon Worcestershire sauce
drop of Tabasco

113

Make the dressing by combining all the ingredients (except lettuce) and mixing thoroughly.

Remove outer leaves of the lettuce (after washing and draining the heads). You can save these outer leaves and use them another time for a tossed green salad. Carefully remove cores from the bottom of the lettuce heads without disturbing the shape of the head. Place the heads on chilled individual salad plates and spoon some of the dressing over each one.

To prepare ahead of time: The dressing can be made several days ahead. The lettuce can be washed, drained, and chilled in the morning.

SLICED TOMATO AND RED ONION SALAD [serves 12]

10 or 12 fresh ripe tomatoes, sliced	salt and pepper
2 or 3 red onions, thinly sliced	French dressing (see recipe on p. 112)

Alternate sliced tomatoes and sliced onions in a large serving dish. Season lightly with salt and pepper. Spoon on French dressing and serve.

To prepare ahead of time: This can be prepared in the morning. Cover tightly with plastic wrap and keep refrigerated until time to serve.

WATERCRESS AND CHERRY TOMATO SALAD
[serves 6]

2 large bunches of watercress, washed, drained and dried—and heavy stems discarded	1 or 2 green onions, finely chopped
1 basket of cherry tomatoes, cut in quarters	French dressing (use recipe on p. 112 made with lemon juice)

Place cleaned watercress in a salad bowl (having torn it into edible-size portions). Sprinkle with green onion. Place quartered cherry tomatoes lightly on top and around edges of salad bowl. Cover tightly with plastic wrap and chill for at least 1 hour. Just before serving toss with the French dressing and serve.

To prepare ahead of time: The salad can be assembled in the morning and kept covered in the refrigerator until time to serve. Then add French dressing, toss, and serve.

GAZPACHO SALAD [serves about 8]

2 cucumbers, sliced and
    then quartered
1 box of cherry tomatoes,
    cut in halves
1 green pepper, chopped
2 cups finely sliced celery
1 cup sliced radishes
5 green onions, chopped

1¼ cups sliced artichoke
    bottoms (canned are okay)
salt and pepper to taste
1 tablespoon chopped parsley
1 avocado, diced
French dressing (of your choice
    or use recipe on p. 112)
sprigs of watercress

Combine the cucumbers, tomatoes, green pepper, celery, radishes, onions, artichoke bottoms, and season with salt and pepper. Toss with French dressing. Cover and chill. Shortly before serving add the chopped parsley and diced avocado. Serve in small chilled salad bowls and garnish with sprigs of watercress.

To prepare ahead of time: Except for the late addition of the parsley and avocado the salad can be combined the day before or in the morning. Keep covered and refrigerated.

LETTUCE AND FRESH MUSHROOM
SALAD WAGRAM [serves 6]

2 heads of Boston (butter)
    lettuce—washed, dried,
    and chilled
½ pound fresh mushrooms,
    thinly sliced

juice of 1 lemon
French dressing (any favorite
    or use recipe on p. 112)

Tear lettuce and place in salad bowl. Cover tightly with plastic wrap and chill until time to serve. Toss sliced mushrooms with lemon juice and refrigerate (in a separate bowl). Just before serving, sprinkle mushrooms over lettuce. Add French dressing to taste— toss and serve.

To prepare ahead of time: Lettuce and mushrooms can be readied in the morning and kept refrigerated until time to serve. Then proceed as directed above.

PAT ALTMAN'S SERBISCHER SALAT [serves about 8 to 10]

one solid head of cabbage (about 2 pounds)
3 large sour pickles
1 red sweet pepper
½ medium onion, grated

2 teaspoons very good quality paprika
salt and pepper to taste
1 tablespoon sugar
¼ cup vinegar
½ cup salad oil

Grate cabbage. Slice or chop or shred pickles and red sweet pepper to approximate size of grated cabbage. Add seasonings to vinegar and oil, then stir until well combined. Pour over salad, mix, and add salt and pepper to taste. The salad should have a pretty reddish color, so add paprika if necessary.

To prepare ahead of time: This can be made in the morning—and, in fact, was in the Wurst Bar where Pat learned to make this in Berlin. It shrinks somewhat when it rests all day and loses its crispness but becomes smoother and better blended. (The salad can even be made one or two days ahead if desired.)

MUSTARD COLESLAW   [serves 6 to 8]

1 large solid head of cabbage, shredded
4 to 6 green onions, finely chopped
1 green pepper, finely chopped
1 cup mayonnaise
1 teaspoon salt

¼ teaspoon pepper
⅓ cup sugar
juice of 1 or 2 lemons (depends on your taste)
¼ cup red wine vinegar
2 tablespoons Dijon style mustard (generous)

Combine shredded cabbage, green onions, and green pepper in a large bowl. Mix remaining ingredients together and pour over the vegetables. Toss until thoroughly mixed. Cover and chill.

To prepare ahead of time: Even better prepared a day or several days ahead. Keep tightly covered and refrigerated. Stir before using.

RED CABBAGE VINAIGRETTE [serves 6 to 8]

1 large solid red cabbage, shredded	¼ cup red wine vinegar
1 large onion, shredded or grated	1¼ teaspoons salt
	¼ teaspoon pepper
1 green pepper, finely chopped (optional)	2 teaspoons tarragon vinegar (or substitute some dried tarragon to your taste)
juice of 2 lemons	¾ cup salad oil

Combine cabbage, onion, and green pepper in a large bowl. Mix lemon juice, red wine vinegar, sugar, salt, pepper, and tarragon vinegar together until sugar has dissolved. Beat in oil, then pour all over cabbage and stir thoroughly. Cover with plastic wrap and chill.

To prepare ahead of time: Best if made at least one day ahead. It should keep a week in the refrigerator—stir occasionally.

DOROTHY WOLPERT'S SPINACH, BEAN SPROUTS, AND WATERCHESTNUT SALAD [serves 6 to 8]

Definitely in the best-of-all-possible category!

1 pound fresh spinach, washed, dried, and torn into bite-size pieces	1 small can waterchestnuts, sliced
1 to 2 cups fresh bean sprouts, washed and drained	¼ to ½ pound bacon, cooked crisp, then crumbled
	Special salad dressing (see below)

Combine spinach, bean sprouts, and sliced waterchestnuts in a large salad bowl. Top with crumbled bacon. Toss with the *special salad dressing* and serve.

Special salad dressing:

½ cup vinegar	1 medium onion, grated
⅓ cup ketchup	1 cup salad oil
⅓ to ½ cup sugar	

Combine in a bowl. Stir until sugar has dissolved. Store in a jar in the refrigerator. *Do not use a blender for this salad dressing.*

To prepare ahead of time: The salad dressing can, of course, be made many days in advance. The salad itself can be readied in the morning (without the dressing)—covered tightly with plastic wrap—then refrigerated until time to serve. Add dressing at that time.

SPINACH, ROMAINE, AND SESAME SEED SALAD

[serves about 8]

1 head of romaine, washed, dried, and chilled	1 cup coarsely grated Monterey Jack cheese
2 bunches of fresh spinach, washed, dried, stems discarded, then chilled	4 tablespoons toasted sesame seeds
¼ to ½ pound of bacon, cooked until crisp, then crumbled	*Special salad dressing* (see below)

Special salad dressing:

1 ½ tablespoons sugar	2 tablespoons grated onion
½ teaspoon salt	¼ cup white wine vinegar
½ teaspoon dry mustard	1 cup salad oil

Combine sugar, salt, mustard, onion, and vinegar, then stir until sugar has dissolved. Gradually beat in the oil. Store in the refrigerator in a tightly sealed jar.

To make the salad: Combine the spinach and romaine (torn in bite size pieces) in a large salad bowl. Scatter the grated cheese over the salad, then sprinkle with the crumbled bacon, then with the sesame seeds. Just before serving add the dressing, toss, and serve.

To prepare ahead of time: The salad can be assembled in the morning—everything except the dressing—covered tightly with plastic wrap and refrigerated. Add dressing just before serving.

AVOCADO SURPRISE [serves 8]

4 avocados
2 tart apples, peeled and cut
  in tiny sticks (julienne)
2 cups tiny celery sticks
  (julienne)
½ cup mayonnaise

1 ½ tablespoons lemon juice
pinch of salt
¼ teaspoon tarragon
4 tablespoons chopped
  candied ginger
lettuce

Combine apples, celery, mayonnaise, lemon juice, salt, tarragon, and chopped candied ginger. Cover and chill.

Peel avocados and cut each in half. Place each on some lettuce and fill with the apple-celery mixture. Serve cold.

Note: If desired the avocados can be cut in thirds—this should then serve twelve. This salad is especially good with the game hens on p. 57 or with other poultry dishes. It is excellent too as a luncheon dish by itself.

To prepare ahead of time: The apple-celery filling can be prepared in the morning. Keep covered and refrigerated.

SALADE NIÇOISE FOR TWO

1 small can of tuna, drained,
  then broken into
  largish pieces
1 green pepper, cut in slices
2 small tomatoes, cut in sixths
French dressing (your choice
  or see recipe on p. 112)

lettuce
2 hard-cooked eggs, quartered
6 anchovies
6 ripe olives

Combine tomatoes, green pepper slices, and tuna and toss with some French dressing. Line individual plates or bowls with lettuce and divide tuna mixture on the lettuce. Top with the anchovies and garnish with the olives and quartered eggs.

This is very good with potato salad vinaigrette served on the side (see recipe on p. 120).

Note: To serve more guests just double, triple, etc. the quantities.

To prepare ahead of time: The obvious: eggs can be cooked the day before; the vegetables can be readied in the morning.

POTATO SALAD VINAIGRETTE

boiling potatoes
salt and pepper to taste
chopped green onions

chopped fresh parsley
French dressing
(see recipe on p. 112)

Cook potatoes until tender but not mushy. Drain, cool slightly, then peel and slice them into a bowl. Sprinkle with salt and pepper, green onions and parsley. While potatoes are still a little warm, add French dressing (to your taste) and mix gently but thoroughly. Cool, then cover and chill.

To prepare ahead of time: Can be done one or two days ahead. Keep well covered and refrigerated.

SWISS CHEESE AND EGG SALAD   [serves 8 to 12]

This has eye appeal as well as taste—especially useful as part of a buffet supper menu.

1 pound imported Swiss
    cheese (cut into small
    sticks about 1 inch long
    and about ¼ inch thick)
14 hard-cooked eggs
salt and pepper to taste

1 teaspoon dry mustard
1 cup sour cream
1 cup Durkee's dressing
chopped parsley
paprika

Set aside 2 of the hard-cooked eggs. You'll need them later for the garnish.

Chop remaining eggs and combine with the cheese sticks, salt, pepper, sour cream, dry mustard, and Durkee's dressing. Taste for seasoning, adding more Durkee's dressing if desired. Spoon into an attractive bowl or platter. Decorate the top with a design made by sprinkling the following in alternating rows: sieved egg yolk, chopped egg whites, paprika, and parsley. Cover with plastic wrap and chill until time to serve.

To prepare ahead of time: This can be made the day before. Keep well covered and refrigerated.

GRAPEFRUIT, AVOCADO, AND DATE SALAD

[serves 4]

1 avocado, peeled and sliced
2 grapefruit, peeled and
    segments removed with-
    out any of the pith

lettuce
8 to 12 dates, pitted and
    coarsely chopped
grapefruit juice or orange juice

Line individual salad plates with lettuce. Place avocado slices and grapefruit segments on top. Sprinkle with dates and spoon some grapefruit or orange juice over all.

To prepare ahead of time: Grapefruit segments can be readied the day before. Keep covered and refrigerated.

ORANGE AND CUCUMBER SALAD

[serves about 8]

5 large sweet oranges, peeled
    and sliced
3 cucumbers, peeled and
    sliced

red lettuce (or any other
    lettuce of your choice)
orange juice mixed with a
    little lemon juice

Line a platter with the red lettuce. (Or if you prefer this can be served on individual salad plates.) Alternate orange and cucumber slices. Spoon the orange-lemon juice mixture over all and chill.

To prepare ahead of time: This can be done in the morning. Cover tightly with plastic wrap and keep refrigerated until time to serve.

WALDORF SALAD WITH GINGER AND RAISINS

[serves about 6]

6 tart apples, peeled then
    sliced or diced
2 cups of chopped celery
½ cup candied ginger,
    chopped

½ cup raisins, soaked in hot
    water, then drained and
    dried on paper towels
1 cup walnuts, coarsely chopped
a little salt
⅓ cup orange juice
mayonnaise to taste

Combine all ingredients and chill for several hours.

To prepare ahead of time: This can be prepared the day before or in the morning. Cover tightly with plastic wrap and keep refrigerated. Stir gently before serving.

NONESUCH FRUIT SALAD [serves 10]

A sumptuous yet cooling accompaniment to hot, spicy dishes such as curries, nasi-goreng, or my version of "Country Captain Chicken" on p. 54.

1 fresh pineapple, cut in long, thick slices	2 cups shredded coconut (canned is fine)
5 large bananas, each cut in 4 chunks	fresh grapes or raspberries or strawberries
2 cups sour cream	lettuce (Boston or other)

This salad can be served either on individual plates or from one large platter. In either case arrange lettuce so that it forms cups to hold the fruit.

Spread the banana chunks thickly with sour cream, then roll them in the coconut. Both the sour cream and coconut coatings should be very generous.

In each lettuce cup arrange two slices of pineapple and two of the sour cream and coconut covered banana chunks. Over the top of each scatter a few grapes or raspberries or strawberries (or all three). (Fruit should be well chilled before arranging the salads.)

Note: If fresh pineapple is unavailable, use sliced oranges as a substitute.

To prepare ahead of time: Fruit can be readied in the morning—including the coating of the banana chunks. Chill each fruit separately. Arrange salads shortly before serving.

Breads, Rolls and Coffee Cakes

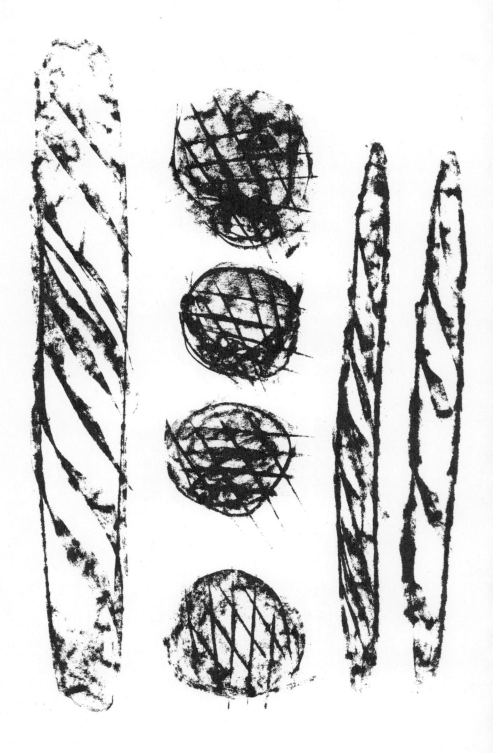

Breads, Rolls and Coffee Cakes

LIGHT, CRUSTY RYE BREAD

[makes 2 large loaves, or 4 small ones]

Designed to be reminiscent of a crunchy crusted light rye bread we ate at La Belle Terrasse in Copenhagen.

2 packages dry yeast
⅔ cup warm water
1 tablespoon sugar
1 tablespoon salt
2 cups warm water
2½ cups rye flour (do not sift, but measure by spooning flour very lightly into measuring cup)

6 cups sifted white flour (all purpose)
3 tablespoons caraway seeds
1 egg white mixed with a tablespoon of water, then beaten slightly
Kosher-style salt (for sprinkling on top of loaves)

Dissolve yeast in the ⅔ cup warm water, then stir in sugar and salt. Place this with the additional 2 cups of warm water in a large bowl and gradually beat in all of the rye flour and as much of the white flour as is necessary to make a very stiff dough. Turn out and knead thoroughly on a floured board, adding more flour as needed. (This can also be done with an electric dough hook if you have one.) Beat or knead in the caraway seeds. Place dough in a greased bowl and cover. Let rise until almost double in bulk—will take 45 minutes or longer. Punch down and turn out on a floured board. Divide dough into 2 or 4 portions (depending on size you desire) and set them aside to "relax" for about 4 or 5 minutes. Shape portions into long loaves and place on baking pans that have been heavily covered with corn meal. Score tops of loaves and brush with the egg white mixture. Let rise about 30 minutes, brush again with egg white and sprinkle with coarse salt.

Bake at 400° for about 30 minutes, reduce heat to 300° and bake about another 20 to 25 minutes. Remove and cool on racks.

Note: Delicious served hot with icy cold sweet butter. It is also good served at room temperature. If there is any left a few days later, slice, butter it, and toast it slowly in the oven until crisp.

To prepare ahead of time: This can be baked the day before. Refrigerate in plastic bags. Reheat to crisp the crust before serving.

To freeze: Like most breads this kind freezes very well. Defrost, then reheat in the oven to crisp the crust.

SALLY LUNN (MY VERSION)

Has the texture of cake—the taste of a light, light bread.

1 package of dry yeast	¼ cup sugar
¼ cup warm water	1 teaspoon salt
2 tablespoons sugar	3 eggs (cold)
½ cup butter	4 cups sifted flour
¾ cup milk	(1 pound)

Sprinkle yeast on the ¼ cup warm water in a small bowl. Add the 2 tablespoons of sugar and stir until yeast is dissolved. Melt butter, add milk, then add the ¼ cup sugar and salt. Stir over moderate heat until sugar and salt have dissolved. Beat eggs in a large bowl. Add milk mixture. Test to make sure it is lukewarm, then add dissolved yeast and stir. Beat in flour vigorously. Cover and let rise until doubled (takes about 1 to 1½ hours). Beat again, then pour into a greased 10-inch tube pan (angel food pan or bundt pan) and let rise again until doubled (about 30 to 45 minutes). Bake at 350° for approximately 40 to 45 minutes. Remove from pan and serve hot with plenty of butter. (Use a serrated knife to cut the bread.)

To prepare ahead of time: This can be baked the day before. Cool, then wrap in foil and refrigerate. Several hours before serving bring to room temperature still wrapped in foil, then reheat (in foil) in a 350° oven.

To freeze: Yes, this freezes. Cool, then wrap very thoroughly in foil. Before serving, defrost completely, then reheat in a 350° oven in its foil wrapping.

SESAME SEED DINNER ROLLS [makes 3 to 4 dozen]

2 packages dry yeast
½ cup warm water
1 teaspoon sugar
½ cup milk, lukewarm
⅓ cup melted shortening
½ teaspoon salt
¼ cup sugar

3 eggs
4½ cups sifted flour
melted butter
1 egg yolk beaten slightly
    with 1 tablespoon water
sesame seeds

Dissolve yeast in warm water, add the 1 teaspoon sugar and mix thoroughly. Combine milk, melted shortening, salt, and the ¼ cup sugar; stir until salt and sugar have dissolved. Beat eggs in a large bowl, then stir in milk mixture. Test to make sure it is lukewarm, then add dissolved yeast and stir. Beat in flour gradually and vigorously, then turn into a greased bowl. Cover and let rise until double in bulk (about 30 to 45 minutes). Divide dough into six portions. Roll each into an oblong about ¼ inch thick. Spread with melted butter and roll up like a jelly roll. Cut in 1-inch pieces and place on greased baking pans. Using the handle of a knife, press firmly across the middle of each. Let rise about 20 to 30 minutes. Brush with egg yolk mixture and sprinkle with sesame seeds. Bake at 400° for 10 to 12 minutes.

To prepare ahead of time: These can be baked the day before. Cool, then store in plastic bags in the refrigerator. Reheat in a 375° oven.

To freeze: These can be frozen. Cool, then freeze in plastic bags. To serve: defrost, then reheat in a 375° oven.

RYE ROLLS [makes about 3 dozen]

2 packages dry yeast
½ cup warm water
¼ cup butter
½ cup boiling water
1 cup milk
½ cup molasses

1 tablespoon salt
4 cups rye flour (unsifted)
2 cups white flour (unsifted)
1 egg white beaten slightly
    with 1 tablespoon of water
caraway seeds

Dissolve yeast in the ½ cup warm water. Melt butter in the boiling water and add the milk, molasses, and salt. Stir. Test to make sure this is lukewarm, then stir in the dissolved yeast. Gradually beat in the rye flour, then beat in or knead in the white flour. (This can be done with an electric dough hook if you have one.) Place in a greased bowl, cover, and let rise until double in bulk (about 1½ to 2 hours).

Shape dough into about 36 small rolls, oval in shape. Place on lightly greased baking pans (the heavier the pans the better, so the bottoms don't burn—or try placing one pan in another if pans are very light). Brush rolls with egg white mixture and sprinkle with caraway seeds. Let rise again until double—approximately 1 hour. Bake at about 400° for 15 to 20 minutes.

To prepare ahead of time: These can be baked the day before. Cool and refrigerate in plastic bags. Reheat before serving.

To freeze: These can be frozen. Freeze in plastic bags. Reheat before serving.

A HOLIDAY FRUIT YEAST BREAD

1 cup butter
¼ cup milk
4 eggs
⅓ cup sugar
1 tablespoon rum
1 package dry yeast
¼ cup warm water
1 tablespoon sugar
¼ cup raisins
½ cup halved or quartered candied cherries
¼ cup chopped candied orange peel
¼ cup blanched shredded almonds
2½ cups sifted flour
½ teaspoon salt

Melt butter, add milk and set aside. Beat eggs with the ⅓ cup sugar. Dissolve yeast in the ¼ cup warm water and stir in the 1 tablespoon of sugar. Combine all these mixtures add rum and stir. Combine fruit with ½ cup of flour. Combine remaining flour with the salt and gradually beat it into the liquid mixture. Add floured fruit and beat again. Grease a tube pan (angel food or other) and sprinkle with the almonds. Pour or spoon in the batter. Cover and let rise until double in bulk (about 1½ to 2 hours). Place in a preheated 350° oven and immediately turn oven to 400° and bake 10 minutes. Reduce to 375°

and bake another 10 minutes. Reduce to 350° and bake about another 20 to 25 minutes. Remove from oven and remove bread to a rack. Unmold and serve warm or at room temperature.

To prepare ahead of time: This can be baked the day before. Cool, wrap in foil, then refrigerate. Reheat in foil wrapping before serving.

To freeze: Yes, this freezes. Cool, then wrap in foil and freeze. To serve: defrost, then reheat in foil wrapping before serving.

FAMILY STYLE CINNAMON ROLLS [makes about 24]

2 packages dry yeast	4 cups sifted flour
½ cup warm water	½ cup melted butter
¼ cup melted butter	¾ cup brown sugar
½ cup plus 2 tablespoons milk (lukewarm)	2 teaspoons cinnamon
	2 tablespoons water
¼ cup sugar	¼ cup melted butter
1 teaspoon salt	cinnamon and sugar
2 eggs	raisins

Place warm water in a small bowl, sprinkle with the dry yeast and stir until dissolved. Combine butter, milk, ¼ cup sugar, and salt and stir to dissolve sugar and salt. Beat eggs in a large bowl and add milk mixture and test to make sure it is lukewarm, then stir in the dissolved yeast. Add half the flour and beat vigorously. Add remaining flour and beat until dough is smooth. (This can be done with an electric dough hook if you have one.) Cover dough and let rise until double—45 minutes to 1½ hours depending on the temperature of dough and room.

Prepare baking pan: Combine the ½ cup melted butter, brown sugar, cinnamon, and the 2 tablespoons of water and cook for a few minutes until smooth and slightly thickened. Pour this into a baking pan about 9″ by 14″ by 2½″.

Prepare rolls: Turn dough on to a floured board and knead for half a minute, then divide into two portions. Let dough "relax" for 5 to 10 minutes. Then roll each portion out to a thickness of about ¼ inch.

Spread with melted butter, sprinkle with cinnamon and sugar and raisins, and then roll up like a jelly roll. Cut each roll into 12 slices and place them cut side down in the prepared pan. Let rise until double in bulk—about 30 minutes or so—and bake at 400° for 10 minutes, then at 350° for about 20 to 30 minutes.

Remove from oven and cool in pan about 1 or 2 minutes, then turn upside down on waxed paper letting the brown sugar glaze run over the rolls.

To prepare ahead of time: These can be baked the day before. Store in the refrigerator wrapped in foil. Reheat before serving.

To freeze: Yes, these can be frozen. Wrap in foil. Defrost, then reheat before serving.

DANISH PASTRY WITH FOUR VARIATIONS

Really not difficult if you set aside a small part of two days to do the work. Make the dough and fillings on one day . . . roll, fill, and bake on another.

Basic pastry (the dough)

1 pound butter (slightly cooler than room temperature)	¼ teaspoon mace
	¼ teaspoon cinnamon
⅓ cup sifted flour (1½ ounces)	1 teaspoon vanilla
	1 teaspoon lemon extract
2 packages dry yeast	4 cups sifted flour
½ cup warm water	(1 pound)
½ cup lukewarm milk	1¾ cups sifted cake flour
1 cup eggs (4 or 5)	(6 ounces)
⅓ cup sugar (3 ounces)	1 egg beaten slightly with
1 teaspoon salt	1 tablespoon of water
2 tablespoons honey	(to be used as an egg wash in all four variations)

General hints: The Danish pastry in its uncooked state will weigh about 4 pounds. You will use about 1 pound per variation, that is, a quarter portion of the raw dough.

After pastries have been rolled, filled, and placed on baking pans do not let them rise too much; less is better than more in this case. Pastries only need to rise until slightly puffy—unless they are very cold, about 30 to 40 minutes should do it.

Preparing the dough: Mix the 1 pound of butter and the ⅓ cup flour to a paste (either with a wooden spoon or with a dough hook if you have one). Spread in a foil pan and chill for about 20 minutes. This is the butter-paste.

Sprinkle yeast on warm water and stir to dissolve. Beat eggs with the sugar, milk, salt, honey, mace, cinnamon, vanilla, and lemon extract. Add dissolved yeast. Gradually beat in the two kinds of flour. Turn into a floured pan and chill about 20 minutes. This is the flour-dough.

Roll out flour-dough into a rectangle about 12″ by 18″ and mark in thirds. Place half of the butter-paste in the center. Fold one third of the flour-dough on top of this. Spread remaining third on top of this.

Turn dough so that the open ends face you and roll out again—this time into a rectangle about 18″ by 24″. Fold both ends to the middle then close like a book—this is called folding the dough in fourths. Turn dough again so that ends face you and repeat this last step. Wrap in waxed paper and chill for 30 to 45 minutes.

Remove pastry from refrigerator and roll again into a rectangle about 18″ by 24″ and fold in fourths as you did previously.

Turn pastry around so that open ends face you and roll out dough into a rectangle about 12″ by 30″. This time fold in thirds. Wrap well in waxed paper and chill overnight. If dough seems to rise too much or too rapidly in the refrigerator, just press it down with the palms of your hands.

Danish Pastry Variation I—Almond Coffee Cake Ring

¼ of the basic pastry (about 1 pound)	⅓ cup brown sugar (pack to measure)
4 ounces almond paste	1 egg
¼ cup butter (room temperature)	¼ cup sifted flour

Cream almond paste with the butter and sugar, making sure to press out all the lumps. Then beat in the egg and stir in the flour.

Roll out pastry into a rectangle about ¼ inch thick. Roll up like a jelly roll along the longest side. Arrange roll in a circular way—crown shape—and place in a greased angel food pan. Press ends together firmly. Brush with egg wash. Let rise until somewhat puffy. Bake at 350° for about 35 to 45 minutes. Remove ring from pan and cool on a rack.

Danish Pastry Variation II—Cinnamon-Raisin Snails

[makes about 1 dozen]

¼ of the basic pastry	cinnamon and sugar
(about 1 pound)	raisins

Roll out pastry into a rectangle about ¼ inch thick. Brush with egg wash. Sprinkle with cinnamon-sugar and with raisins. Fold pastry in half, then cut in 1-inch strips. Twist the strips, then roll each into coils (like snails) and place on greased pans. Be sure to tuck the end of each coil underneath so that coils will stay in place. Brush with egg wash. Let rise until slightly puffy. Bake at 375° for 15 to 20 minutes.

Danish Pastry Variation III—Pecan Rolls   [makes 10 to 12]

¼ of the basic pastry	cinnamon-sugar
(about 1 pound)	melted butter
½ cup chopped pecans	brown sugar
pecan halves	

Roll out pastry into a rectangle about ¼ inch thick. Brush with egg wash and sprinkle with cinnamon-sugar and with the chopped pecans. Roll up from the longest side and cut into 10 or 12 pieces.

Brush muffin tins very generously with melted butter and sprinkle the bottom of each with 1 or 2 teaspoons of brown sugar. Place pastry slices in each. Brush with egg wash and let rise until slightly puffy. Bake at 375° for about 15 to 20 minutes. Turn out upside down on waxed paper immediately after removing from oven.

Danish Pastry Variation IV—Honey Almond Coffee Cake

¼ of the basic pastry	¼ cup honey
(about 1 pound)	⅓ cup sugar
¼ cup butter	1 cup sliced almonds

Roll or pat the pastry into a 9- or 10-inch round and fit it into the bottom of a well-greased 9- or 10-inch spring form pan.

Combine butter, honey, and sugar and bring to a boil. Stir in almonds. Remove from heat and cool until just warm to the touch. Spread or spoon this mixture on top of the dough in the pan. Let rise until slightly puffy. Bake at 375° for about 25 minutes. Cool in pan for about 10 or 15 minutes, then remove and finish cooling on a cake rack.

To prepare ahead of time: The pastries can be baked the day before you plan to serve them. After they are cool put them in plastic bags and refrigerate. Reheat before serving.

To freeze: The pastries can be baked and frozen. Place in plastic bags after they are cool and then freeze. Reheat before serving.

ORANGE BREAD [makes 2 loaves]

Orange peel from 4 oranges (use a potato peeler so that you get only the orange part)
½ cup water
1 cup sugar

4 cups sifted flour
½ teaspoon salt
3 teaspoons baking powder
⅓ cup butter or shortening
2 eggs
1 cup milk

Place orange peel in a saucepan and cover with boiling water. Boil until tender—about 15 to 20 minutes. Remove and drain. Cut in small strips or chop into small pieces. Boil the ½ cup of water and the 1 cup of sugar together until it spins a thread. Add orange peel and cook uncovered for about 8 to 10 minutes. Remove from heat and cool.

Sift dry ingredients together. Place in a bowl, add and cut in the butter or shortening. Beat eggs and milk together, add to flour mixture and stir only until blended. Stir in the cooked orange peel—syrup and all—and blend again. Spoon into two loaf pans which have been greased and floured. Bake at 350° for 50 to 60 minutes. Remove from pans and cool on racks.

Serve this bread the following day if possible. Slice thinly and spread with sweet butter. Good at tea time—I like it for breakfast with my coffee.

To prepare ahead of time: Yes, by all means, do bake this the day before. It slices more easily and tastes much better. After loaves are cool wrap in foil and refrigerate. Bring to room temperature before serving.

To freeze: Cool, then wrap in foil and freeze. Defrost and bring to room temperature before serving.

CORNBREAD [serves 6 to 8]

1 cup corn meal	1 egg
1 cup sifted flour	1 cup milk
2 tablespoons sugar	⅓ cup melted butter
3 teaspoons baking powder	(or salad oil)
1 teaspoon salt	

Combine dry ingredients in a bowl. Beat egg, milk, and melted butter together. Add to dry ingredients and stir only until blended. Don't overmix. Pour into a greased 9-inch square pan (or fill greased muffin tins about ⅔ full). Bake at 400° for 20 to 25 minutes.

Note: This is a useful recipe for the turkey stuffing on p. 60.

To prepare ahead of time: Best baked and eaten fresh—however—really quite good reheated the next day.

To freeze: Best way to freeze this is as cornbread muffins. As soon as they are cool place them in plastic bags and freeze. Reheat in the oven before serving.

PEACHY MUFFINS [makes 1 dozen]

¼ cup softened butter	1 ¾ cup sifted flour
⅓ cup sugar	½ teaspoon salt
1 egg broken into a	2 ½ teaspoons baking powder
measuring cup, then	1 cup diced peaches (make
milk added to make	sure they are very well
1 cup	drained)

134

Cream butter and sugar together. Add egg-milk mixture and beat. Sift dry ingredients together and add, stirring only until blended. Do not overmix or beat. Blend in diced peaches. Fill greased muffin tins about ⅔ full. Bake at 400° for 20 to 25 minutes.

To prepare ahead of time: These can be baked the day before. Cool, then put in plastic bags and refrigerate. Reheat before serving.

To freeze: Cool, then put in plastic bags and freeze. Reheat before serving.

BRAN AND MOLASSES MUFFINS   [makes 1 dozen]

1 cup of All-Bran	½ cup raisins
½ cup milk	1 cup sifted flour
½ cup dark molasses	½ teaspoon salt
1 egg	2½ teaspoons baking powder
¼ cup soft butter or	
shortening	

Combine All-Bran, milk and molasses. Let this stand for about 5 minutes. Beat in the egg and butter or shortening. Stir in the raisins. Sift dry ingredients together, then add and stir only until combined. Do not beat. Spoon mixture into greased muffin tins. Bake in a 400° oven for 20 to 25 minutes.

To prepare ahead of time: These can be baked the day before. After they have cooled place in plastic bags and refrigerate. Reheat before serving.

To freeze: Yes, do freeze these. After they are cool place in plastic bags and then freeze. Reheat before serving.

MINCEMEAT MUFFINS [makes 1 dozen]

2 cups sifted flour	¾ cup milk
3 teaspoons baking powder	¼ cup salad oil
½ teaspoon salt	1 egg
3 tablespoons sugar	¾ cup mincemeat (canned)

Sift dry ingredients together and place in a bowl. Beat together the milk, salad oil, egg, and mincemeat. Add liquid mixture to dry ingredients and stir only until combined. Do not beat. Fill greased muffin tins about ¾ full. Bake at 425° for about 20 minutes.

To prepare ahead of time: These can be baked the day before. Store in the refrigerator either in plastic bags or wrapped in foil. Reheat before serving.

To freeze: Cool, then wrap in foil or place in plastic bags. Reheat before serving.

Gâteaux Magnifiques

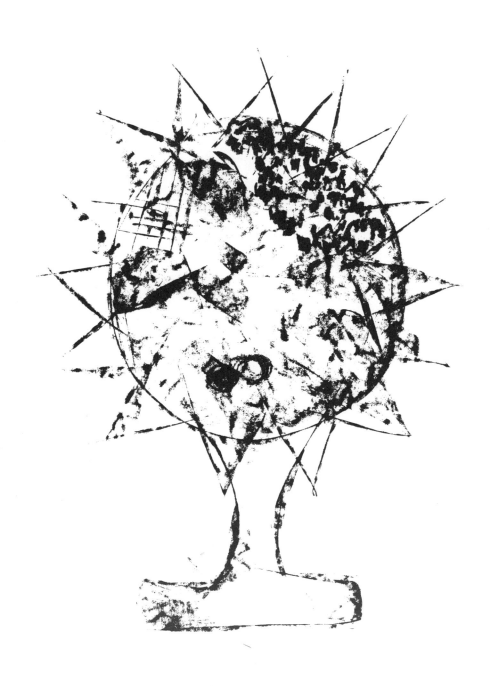

Gâteaux Magnifiques

GÂTEAU PRALINÉ SANS RIVAL [serves about 40]

A lengthy process—but it merits your time if you want to produce an unrivaled masterpiece for an important occasion.

You will need:

4 12-inch *meringue-nut layers* (recipe follows)
2 quarts of *buttercream* recipe on p. 155)

1 ½ cups *praline powder* (recipe on p. 156)
Krokant (also called Nougat paste), recipe follows

Meringue-nut layers:
Please note: This recipe will have to be MADE TWICE to produce the needed 4 layers.

8 egg whites
¼ teaspoon salt
¼ teaspoon cream of tartar
1 ½ cups sugar

1 ½ cups blanched almonds, toasted, then ground in a blender
1 cup filberts, toasted, skins rubbed off, then ground in a blender

Mix ground almonds and filberts with 1 cup of the sugar. Beat egg whites, cream of tartar, and salt until stiff, then gradually beat in remaining ½ cup of sugar. Fold into the nut mixture. Line two large baking sheets with non-sticking silicone paper. (If you are unable to obtain this marvelous paper, then grease the pans with vegetable shortening and dust with flour.) Draw a 12-inch circle on each paper (or greased and floured pans). I use the outer rim of a 12-inch spring form pan as my guide. Divide the meringue-nut mixture on the two circles and spread as evenly as possible. Bake at 275° for about 35 to 40 minutes—until crusty on top but still a little pliable. Remove, invert, and remove paper—or—if using greased and floured pans, loosen meringues with the aid of a large spatula and long knife. Cool.

Now, *repeat this recipe,* thus producing the needed 4 layers.

Krokant (Nougat paste):

1 cup sugar	2 tablespoons water
½ teaspoon lemon juice	⅓ cup blanched almonds, measured then ground

Place sugar, lemon juice, and water in a heavy skillet. Cook and stir over moderate heat until sugar becomes a caramel. Stir in the ground almonds, then pour on to a greased metal cookie sheet. Immediately spread the nougat as thin as possible using a greased metal spatula or knife. While still warm mark and cut the nougat into small diamonds or rectangles approximately 1″ by 2″. Place these on waxed paper and set aside. The best way to store these if making them a day or two ahead of time is between layers of waxed paper in an airtight tin.

To assemble the gâteau: Place buttercream (which you have brought to room temperature) in a large bowl. Whip in the 1½ cups of praline powder. Fill, stack, and frost the 4 meringue-nut layers with this praline buttercream. Decorate top with the krokant diamonds or rectangles. Cover with plastic wrap and chill. Serve cool but not icy cold.

To prepare ahead of time: This can be made and assembled several days ahead—if you have room in your refrigerator to store this gâteau. It must be carefully and completely covered with plastic wrap. Other possibilities: make the separate parts of this gâteau one or two days ahead, then assemble it the day of your party.

To freeze: The buttercream and the praline powder can be frozen. Make certain that they are placed in tightly sealed containers. The entire gâteau can be frozen except for the krokant decorations. Those can be made as directed above a few days before; add before serving. Be sure that the gâteau is thoroughly wrapped if you plan to store it in the freezer.

GÂTEAU DE JOIE [serves about 16]

You will need:

4 rectangular *meringue-nut layers* (see below)
1 quart of *buttercream* (see recipe on p. 155)
chocolate wafers (see below)

1 or 2 teaspoons vanilla
¼ cup *praline powder* (see recipe on p. 156)
3 ounces semi-sweet chocolate, melted

Meringue-nut layers (using the basic recipe on p. 139):

Make a single recipe of the meringue-nut mixture on p. 139. Prepare two very large baking pans as in that recipe, but this time mark each with two rectangles 4 inches by 12 inches—thus making a total of 4. Spread each rectangle with the meringue-nut mixture and bake as directed in the recipe.

Chocolate wafers:

Melt 6 ounces of semi sweet chocolate. Cut out 2- or 2 ½ -inch circles of waxed paper. Spread them thinly with the chocolate and chill. When hardened remove the paper. Keep wafers chilled until ready to use.

To prepare three buttercream mixtures:

1. Whip 1 or 2 teaspoons of vanilla into 1 cup of the prepared buttercream.
2. Whip the ¼ cup praline powder into another 1 cup of the buttercream.
3. Whip the 3 ounces of melted semi-sweet chocolate into the remaining 2 cups of buttercream.

To assemble the gâteau:

Place one of the meringue-nut layers on a serving plate or serving board. Spread with the vanilla buttercream. Top with second meringue-nut layer. Spread this with the praline buttercream. Top with the third meringue-nut layer and spread with half of the chocolate buttercream. Place last meringue-nut layer on top. Frost top and sides of the gâteau with the remaining chocolate buttercream.

Use the chocolate wafers to decorate the gâteau—either press them against the sides and top—or just around the sides. Cover gâteau with plastic wrap and refrigerate until time to serve.

To prepare ahead of time: The chocolate wafers, the buttercream, the praline powder can all be prepared several days ahead and kept refrigerated. The meringue layers can be baked a day or so ahead too. And—if you have room in your refrigerator the entire gâteau can be assembled, covered with plastic wrap and kept refrigerated—several days to a week ahead.

To freeze: The gâteau can be assembled and frozen. Make certain that it is very well wrapped.

LE GRAND GÂTEAU DU CHOCOLAT [serves 24 or more]

You will need:

4 9-inch layers of *chocolate cake* (see recipe below)
chocolate filling (see recipe below)
1 cup of *buttercream* (see recipe on p. 155)

1 or 2 teaspoons powdered coffee dissolved in 2 tablespoons of boiling water
chocolate curls (see recipe below)

Chocolate cake:

4 squares unsweetened chocolate
2 ⅔ cups sifted cake flour
2 ⅔ cups sugar
¾ teaspoon baking powder
2 teaspoons baking soda
1 ¼ teaspoons salt

¾ cup butter (room temperature)
1 cup milk
4 eggs (room temperature)
¾ cup milk
2 teaspoons vanilla

Melt chocolate over low heat, then let it cool. Sift all dry ingredients together and place in a mixing bowl. Add the butter and the 1 cup of milk. Beat with an electric beater on low speed for 1 minute. Add melted chocolate and beat another minute. Add the remaining milk, eggs, and vanilla and beat again on low speed for 1 or 2 minutes. Do not overbeat or cake will be dry and tough. Pour into four 9-inch layer cake pans which have been greased and floured. Bake at 350° for 30 to 35 minutes. Cool on racks for 4 or 5 minutes, then remove from pans and finish cooling.

Chocolate filling:

| 24 ounces dark sweet | 2 cups heavy cream |
| chocolate | 2 teaspoons vanilla |

Melt chocolate slowly over simmering water. Heat cream to the boiling point, then add to melted chocolate and beat vigorously (a wire whisk is best for this). Add vanilla and beat again. Let cool to room temperature, beating occasionally while it cools.

Chocolate curls:

8 ounces semi-sweet chocolate

Melt chocolate, then spread it on the back of two pans each 11″ by 17″. If using different size pans, remember that chocolate must be very thinly spread. Chill until hardened. Remove from refrigerator and after a minute or so make the curls by scraping the chocolate with the aid of a large chef's knife or spatula. Work with only one pan at a time. You will see as you begin to work with the chocolate that there is just the right moment to do the scraping—chocolate is neither too cold and brittle nor too warm and soft. If chocolate is too cold let pan stand at room temperature a minute or so longer; if too soft, return briefly to the refrigerator.

When curls are finished place them on a large dish or in a pan, cover with plastic wrap and keep refrigerated until needed.

Coffee flavored buttercream: Place the 1 cup of buttercream in a bowl, then gradually whip in as much of the dissolved coffee as you like.

To assemble: Split each chocolate cake layer in half—thus you now have 8 layers. Fill each layer with the prepared chocolate filling including the top of the top layer. Cover the sides of the cake after layers have been filled with the coffee buttercream. Press chocolate curls around the sides (that is, into the buttercream). Cover with plastic wrap and chill, but please remember to serve this gâteau at room temperature!

To prepare ahead of time: The entire gâteau can be prepared and assembled as much as a week ahead if you have room in your refrigerator. It must be stored there and must be carefully and completely covered with plastic wrap. There are other do-ahead possibilities. The cakes, the buttercream, the chocolate filling, and the chocolate curls can all be made several days ahead and stored in the refrigerator. Be sure to bring them to room temperature before assembling the gâteau.

To freeze: The entire assembled gâteau can be frozen—be sure it is thoroughly covered with plastic wrap, or even better, with several layers of same. Or, the component parts of the gâteau can be frozen separately. Defrost, bring to room temperature, then assemble the gâteau.

DEUX GÂTEAUX AUX AMANDES (PITHIVIERS)
[serves about 16]

The theory behind this: since you are going to the trouble of making one, why not make two! You can serve them at that largish dinner party you have been thinking about.

You will need:

Puff pastry (1 full recipe on p. 152)

Pithiviers filling (recipe follows) for which you will need: Almond filling (see recipe on p. 157) and Pastry cream (recipe on p. 157)

1 egg beaten with 1 tablespoon of water, to be used as an egg wash

powdered sugar

Pithiviers filling:

⅔ of the Almond filling that you make in the recipe on p. 157 (freeze the rest)

1 cup of Pastry cream recipe on p. 157)

2 tablespoons flour

Blend these three items together gently and thoroughly, then chill until needed.

To make the deux gâteaux: Divide the puff pastry into four portions, then do the following FOR EACH GÂTEAU:

144

1. Roll out one portion of the puff pastry into a 12-inch square (it should be about ⅛ inch thick or possibly a little thicker). Place on a lightly greased, then cold-water-rinsed baking sheet. (This is the bottom crust.)

2. Roll out another portion of pastry the same as the first but into a slightly larger rectangle (this is the top crust) and set aside.

3. Place a half portion of the prepared Pithiviers filling on the center of the first (smaller) rectangle (the bottom crust) and be sure to leave at least 3 inches uncovered around all sides of the bottom crust. Egg wash this exposed pastry. Place top crust over the filling and press top and bottom crusts together firmly.

4. Using a 9-inch flan ring or the outside ring of a 9-inch spring form pan lightly mark out a 9-inch circle, then using this as your guide cut out and around it in a scalloped pattern. Chill for at least 45 minutes.

Filling on bottom crust: After top crust has been added:

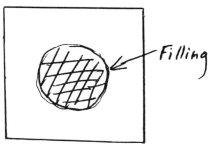
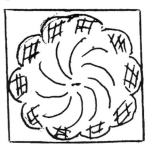

Filling

5. Brush top twice with egg wash, but keep it only on the pastry top—don't let any drip on the sides or on the baking pan. Score the top in a whirl design but don't cut all the way through. (See drawing above.) Cut one ¾ inch gash in the center. Lightly criss-cross the edges.

6. Bake at 400° until it begins to brown (about 10 minutes), then reduce oven to 350° and bake about 35 minutes or a bit longer.

7. Just before the gâteau seems to be completely baked, remove from oven and sprinkle the top (use a sieve) with powdered sugar. Return to a preheated 450° oven and bake 2 to 5 minutes, or until sugar melts and forms a glaze. Watch carefully during this last step so that you don't burn your masterpiece.

8. Serve warmish or at room temperature.

To prepare ahead of time: This can be completely assembled in the morning. Store in the refrigerator. Bake a few hours before serving.

To freeze: I think this is at its best when baked and eaten on the same day. It is, however, really very good after it has been frozen. Defrost completely, then reheat in the oven before serving.

One should keep in mind too that since several of the component parts of this recipe can be frozen—the puff pastry and the Almond filling—it is not such a time consuming task to prepare this the morning of your party.

GÂTEAU AUX TROIS COULEURS [serves about 16]

You will need:

1 10-inch *Sponge cake* (see recipe below)
3 9-inch layers of *Sponge cake* (recipe for the 10-inch layer will have to be repeated, see below)
¼ cup sifted unsweetened cocoa
red food color

1½ cups light rum
½ cup cognac (or brandy)
1 cup apricot jam (about)
1 cup seedless raspberry jam (about)
Butter icing (recipe follows)
Mock Fondant icing (recipe follows)

Sponge Cake: Please note: The ingredients will have to be repeated to make the other three layers.

8 eggs (room temperature)
1 cup sugar
1¼ cups sifted flour

¼ teaspoon salt
¾ teaspoon baking powder

For the 10-inch cake: Beat eggs until thick and light, then gradually beat in the sugar and beat until thick. Sift flour, salt, and baking powder together three times, then fold lightly into the egg mixture. Pour into a greased and floured 10-inch spring form pan and bake at 325° for 30 to 40 minutes—or until surface springs back when touched.

For the 3 9-inch layers: Repeat the ingredients and the beating procedure that you used for the 10-inch cake. This time, however, divide the batter equally into three parts. Tint one pink (carefully adding a little red food color). Fold sifted cocoa into the second. Leave third plain. Place these three mixtures into three greased and floured 9-inch layer cake pans and bake at 325° for about 20 minutes. Remove from pans and cool on racks.

To assemble the gâteau: Slice off a ½ inch layer from the top of the large cake. Carefully cut around the inside of cake, ½ inch from edge and bottom—removing the insides. Spread inside of this cake shell with apricot jam.

Dice the 3 9-inch layers plus the insides that you just removed from the large cake and place in a large bowl. Moisten well with all the rum and cognac and toss. Place the large cake box back in the 10-inch spring form pan— this is necessary to keep it firmly in place. Pack this box with the diced and moistened cake cubes, pressing down firmly. Now, spread the inside of the top you sliced off the large cake with the raspberry jam and place this on top of the packed cake box. Using a plate or something similar, plus a weight, keep this weighted down overnight if possible—but at the very least for several hours.

Butter Icing:

⅓ cup butter (soft)	2 egg whites
1 pound powdered sugar (sifted)	1 tablespoon rum

Cream butter and sugar—or better—beat with an electric mixer. Beat in egg whites and rum until very smooth.

Mock Fondant icing:

½ cup sugar	2 cups sifted powdered sugar
2 tablespoons water	(about)
⅛ teaspoon cream of tartar	red food coloring

Combine sugar, water, and cream of tartar in a saucepan. Dissolve and stir slowly, then bring to a boil. Remove from heat and cool until just warm. Stir in powdered sugar until a fondant icing consistency is achieved. Tint a delicate pink using a tiny bit of red food color.

To ice the gâteau: Remove outer edge of the spring form pan but leave cake on the bottom part of the pan. Cover sides and top with a thin layer of raspberry jam. Spread the sides of the cake with the butter icing. Cover the top with the pink fondant icing. Cover with plastic wrap and keep refrigerated. Bring to room temperature before serving.

To prepare ahead of time: As you can already see, much of this must be done at least one day ahead. The entire gâteau can be completed 10 days ahead—wrapped very carefully and completely and kept refrigerated until a few hours before serving.

To freeze: Sponge cakes freeze admirably. I don't recommend freezing the gâteau after it has been completely assembled.

GÂTEAU MILLEFEUILLE [serves about 12]

You will need:

1 full recipe of *puff pastry,* see p. 152
Special filling (recipe follows)
Vanilla icing (recipe follows)

apricot jam (put through a sieve)
sliced almonds, toasted
a few chopped pistachio nuts

Special filling:

2 whole eggs
2 egg yolks
¾ cup sugar
pinch of salt
½ cup flour

2 cups milk, heated
1½ tablespoons gelatin
¼ cup cold water
2 teaspoons vanilla
1½ cups heavy cream, whipped

Beat eggs and egg yolks with the sugar and salt, then gradually beat in the flour, adding a little of the milk. Add remaining milk and place this mixture in the top of a double boiler. Cook and stir until thickened. Soak gelatin in the cold water, then add to the custard while it is still hot. Stir until dissolved. Remove from heat, add vanilla, and cool over ice, stirring, until it begins to thicken. Now fold in the whipped cream. Chill until time to use.

Vanilla icing:

1 tablespoon butter
2 tablespoons milk

sifted powdered sugar
1 teaspoon vanilla

Melt butter, add milk and heat only until barely warm. Remove from heat and gradually stir in the sifted powdered sugar—enough to make it of spreading consistency. Add vanilla and stir.

To prepare gâteau: Divide puff pastry into 4 portions. Roll each one into a large square—about 12 inches or more on each side. Cut into 12-inch rounds and place them on large wet baking sheets. You can use the trimmings for another purpose. Chill at least 15 minutes—longer is better. Place in a 450° oven and bake for 10 minutes. Reduce heat to 350° and continue baking until golden brown—possibly another 20 to 30 minutes. Pastry must be thoroughly baked and crisp but not burned.

A few hours before serving: Spread filling on three of the baked puff pastry rounds and stack them. Top with the fourth pastry round and frost that one with the vanilla icing. Sprinkle with chopped pistachios. Trim edges of the gâteau, then coat the sides with apricot jam and cover with the toasted sliced almonds. Chill until time to serve. The gâteau is at its crispest best if you do not fill it too far ahead of time. Bring to the table and slice it with a long, serrated knife.

To prepare ahead of time: The puff pastry can be made several days ahead—but bake it the morning of the party. The filling can be made the day before.

To freeze: In this case the only part that can be frozen successfully is the unbaked puff pastry; this in itself is a major part of the work for this gâteau.

ARABESQUE DE MERINGUE [serves 12 to 14]

16 egg whites	3 to 4 boxes of strawberries
4 cups sugar	sugar (to sweeten strawberries)
½ teaspoon salt	1½ quarts vanilla ice cream
2 teaspoons vinegar	1½ cups whipping cream,
2 teaspoons vanilla	whipped
Grand Marnier liqueur	

First meringue mixture: Beat 8 of the egg whites until they are stiff enough to stand in soft peaks. Continue beating, adding very gradually 1 ½ cups sugar. Beat in ¼ teaspoon salt, 1 teaspoon vinegar, and 1 teaspoon vanilla. Now, fold in ½ cup sugar.

Draw three 9-inch circles on waxed paper and one 8-inch circle. Place each of these on a cookie sheet.

> 1st: Fill one of the 9-inch rings in completely with meringue, about ¼ to ½ inch thickness. This will serve as the base.
> 2nd: Pipe out two rings about 1 ½ inches wide by 1 ½ inches high on the two remaining 9-inch circles.
> 3rd: Pipe out a cover of rosettes and swirls or whatever, on the 8-inch circle—this must be solid so as to serve as the cover for the gâteau.

Bake these meringue circles at 250° for about 1 hour or longer—until the paper can be easily removed. If necessary, return them to the oven to dry longer.

Second meringue mixture: Repeat the procedure for the first meringue mixture, using the remaining 8 egg whites, 2 cups sugar, ¼ teaspoon salt, 1 teaspoon vinegar, and 1 teaspoon vanilla.

After this has been prepared use part of it to cement the two baked 9-inch rings together on the 9-inch base. Then using a spatula smooth some of the meringue both inside and outside the gâteau so that it looks like one large, smooth, hollow cake. With the remaining meringue, pipe the sides and outside bottom edge with rosettes, swirls, etc. Return to the 250° oven and bake for about 1 hour or longer, or until as dry as you like it. Remove from oven and cool thoroughly. (Of course the 8-inch rosette-cover does not need this second baking.)

Filling: Sweeten strawberries to your taste and add some Grand Marnier. Chill. Whip the cream and chill. Scoop ice cream into small portions and keep in freezer.

To serve: Fill the hollow of the gâteau with a few of the strawberries, then a little ice cream, then some whipped cream and cover with the rosette-cover. Arrange the remaining strawberries, ice cream, and whipped cream in three bowls. Bring all to the table. Cut and serve each guest a portion of the arabesque and serve additional strawberries, ice cream, and whipped cream with each on the side of the dessert plate. (Hint: use dessert plates of generous size—or—use your dinner plates.) I find it easiest to cut this dessert with the aid of a long, heavy, serrated bread knife.

To prepare ahead of time: The meringue arabesque can be baked one or two days ahead of time. After it has cooled wrap it in plastic wrap or waxed paper and leave at room temperature.

To freeze: The meringue arabesque can be frozen—but not for more than a week. Remove from freezer about 30 or 40 minutes before serving, then proceed as in the above recipe.

LE BEAU GÂTEAU [serves about 10]

You will need:

3 9-inch layers of *Genoise cake* (recipe follows)
½ cup sugar
½ cup water
⅓ cup kirsch

2 cups *pastry cream* (double the recipe on p. 157)
Macaroon mixture (recipe follows)
raspberry jam (seedless)

Genoise cake:

6 eggs
1½ cups sugar
1½ cups sifted cake flour

1½ teaspoons baking powder
5 tablespoons butter (melted and cooled)

Be sure to allow the melted butter to cool. Sift flour and baking powder together three times and leave it in the sifter. Beat the eggs with an electric mixer until light, then gradually add the sugar, continuing to beat until thickened and very light in color (about 8 to 10 minutes). Sift flour-baking powder into this gradually, folding it gently in at the same time. Pour and cut in the butter on top of batter—then fold in with a few quick strokes. Pour into three 9-inch layer cake pans with removable bottoms. (Or lacking those, grease bottoms of pans, line with waxed paper circles, and grease again.) Bake at 350° for 15 to 20 minutes. Cakes will be done if the surface springs back when touched. Remove from oven, then from pans, and cool on racks.

Macaroon mixture:

4 ounces almond paste
½ cup sugar

2 egg whites (about)

151

Beat almond paste with the sugar first to remove lumps, then gradually beat in the egg whites—need the mixture only a little softer than for almond macaroons.

To assemble the gâteau: Boil the ½ cup sugar and the ½ cup water together—stirring to dissolve sugar. Remove from heat and add the kirsch.

Place one layer of the genoise cake on an ovenproof plate. Brush with ⅓ of the kirsch syrup. Spread with about ¼ of the pastry cream. Place second layer on top and brush that with ⅓ of the syrup, then with ¼ the pastry cream. Top with third layer, brush with remaining kirsch syrup and now, using all the remaining pastry cream, cover the entire cake.

Place the macaroon mixture in a pastry bag with a no. 2 round tube and decorate the top by piping out strips 1 inch apart in a lattice pattern. Place little rosettes around the outer edge. Bake at 400° for 15 to 20 minutes. If necessary you can brown the top for a minute or so under the broiler unit.

Remove from oven and cool for about 10 or 15 minutes. Fill the open spaces within the macaroon lattice top with raspberry jam using either a spoon or a small pastry bag made out of parchment paper. Chill for several hours and then serve.

To prepare ahead of time: The cakes can be baked the day before and the pastry cream can be prepared the day before. Assemble and bake the gâteau the morning of the party.

To freeze: The genoise layer cakes can be frozen. Freeze them first to a somewhat solid state, then wrap in foil—this will avoid squashing the cakes when you wrap them.

PUFF PASTRY   [makes 3½ pounds]

1¼ pounds butter (5 sticks)
1¼ cups sifted cake flour
    (4 ounces)
4 cups sifted ordinary flour
    (1 pound)

1 teaspoon salt
1½ cups ice water

Special note: You will notice as you read the directions that the pastry must be rolled many times. The most useful hint for making puff pastry that I can give is to remember to use a very generous amount of flour when rolling the pastry—don't worry about the excess. But do remember to use a pastry brush to brush off all excess flour as you fold the dough—thereby enabling the layers to stick together.

Butter paste: Mix butter and cake flour together in a bowl with a wooden spoon or with an electric dough hook. (Butter should be slightly soft but not warm.) Chill for 5 or 10 minutes—should be cool but not hardened.

Flour paste: Mix ordinary flour and salt together in a bowl, then add ice water and stir until combined (do not beat or overmix). Chill for about 10 minutes.

To roll and fold pastry (see illustration on p. 154):
Step 1:
   A. Roll out flour paste to a rectangle about 12 by 18 inches and mark in thirds. Place half of butter paste in the center.
   B. Fold one third over center. Place remaining butter paste on top.
   C. Fold over with remaining third. Pat down lightly. Wrap in waxed paper and chill 30 to 45 minutes.

Step 2:
   A. Turn the dough so that one side with open edges faces you as you begin rolling. This is the position the dough must be in whenever you roll the pastry.
   B. Roll out into a rectangle about 18 by 30 inches.
   C. Fold ends to middle.
   D. Then fold double (just like a book) and press gently but firmly.

Step 3: Turn dough so edges again face you and repeat Step 2. Wrap in waxed paper and chill again for 30 to 45 minutes.

Step 4: Repeat Step 2, then without chilling:

Step 5: Repeat Step 2 and chill for at least several hours—overnight is better.

Note: As you can see, pastry is first rolled and folded in thirds, then it is rolled and folded four times in fourths.

153

STEP 1

A.

12"

18"

HALF OF BUTTER PASTE

Here — Here

B.

C.

STEP 2

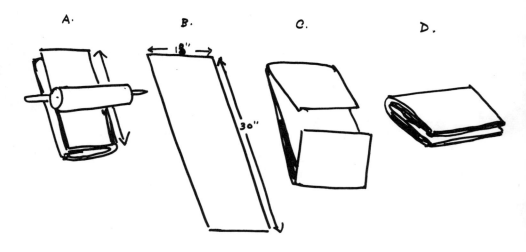

A.

B.

18"

30"

C.

D.

To prepare ahead of time: The pastry is best prepared a day ahead. It will keep in the refrigerator (well wrapped) for several days.

To freeze: The puff pastry freezes. I usually divide a batch into two portions. Wrap in plastic wrap or waxed paper, then in several layers of foil. Best to defrost the pastry overnight in the refrigerator.

BUTTERCREAM [makes 2 quarts]

For any serious *pâtissier* or *pâtissière* buttercream is a must. This one can be frozen—so by all means keep some on hand.

2 cups sugar (1 pound)	1 pound and 6 ounces of
¾ cup water	butter—use half sweet
⅛ teaspoon cream of tartar	and half regular (this is
⅛ teaspoon salt	5 sticks of butter plus
8 egg whites	2 tablespoons)

Put sugar, water, cream of tartar, and salt in a heavy saucepan and stir over low heat until sugar has dissolved. Bring slowly to a boil, then cook WITHOUT STIRRING until mixture reaches the soft ball stage (when a few drops of syrup in cold water form a soft ball). While the syrup is cooking remove any sugar grains that form around the side of the pan with the aid of wet paper towels wrapped around a fork.

As soon as syrup has reached the soft ball stage remove from heat and IMMEDIATELY beat egg whites until stiff but not dry. (You can have them ready to be beaten in your electric mixer.) Add hot syrup very slowly, beating constantly, until all syrup has been added. Now, continue beating until this meringue has cooled to room temperature. Gradually beat in the butter. Flavor and use as desired.

Note: You will notice that as you beat in the butter the mixture will look somewhat peculiar, but keep going—that certain moment will be reached where the two "catch" and you can see the beautiful texture of buttercream achieved.

To prepare ahead of time: This can be made several days ahead. Keep refrigerated. Bring to room temperature before adding flavorings and whisk with a wire whisk. If it looks a little "curdled," just whisk in 1 teaspoon of boiling water—it will "catch" again.

To freeze: Yes, thank goodness, this does freeze. Defrost and bring to room temperature before using. Follow directions under *To prepare ahead of time*. (I find it most convenient to freeze this in about 1 or 2 cup quantities.)

PRALINE POWDER

2 cups sugar	2 cups blanched almonds

Place sugar in a large heavy skillet (one of the cast iron skillets is perfect for this). Melt sugar slowly to a caramel over moderate heat, stirring occasionally. Add almonds and stir over low heat until they are completely coated with the caramel. Pour at once into a lightly greased metal pan. Let it cool and harden. Break it up, then whirl in a blender doing a small portion at a time.

To prepare ahead of time: This praline powder will keep for several months in the refrigerator if kept in tightly sealed jars.

To freeze: Freeze in containers that can be tightly sealed.

ALMOND FILLING

8 ounces almond paste	2 eggs
1 cup sugar (8 ounces)	1 teaspoon vanilla
½ cup butter (¼ pound)	2 tablespoons rum or cognac

Cream almond paste and sugar together to remove lumps, then beat in the butter. Lastly beat in eggs, vanilla, and rum or cognac. Chill.

To prepare ahead of time: This can be made several days ahead and kept refrigerated.

To freeze: This can be frozen.

PASTRY CREAM

3 egg yolks	pinch of salt
⅓ cup sugar (2 ounces)	1 cup milk
2 tablespoons cornstarch	1 teaspoon vanilla
(½ ounce)	

Beat egg yolks with sugar in the top of a double boiler. Then beat in the cornstarch and salt. Heat milk to the boiling point. Add to yolk mixture beating constantly. (Use a wire whisk for this task.) Cook over simmering water, stirring constantly, until mixture is very thick. Remove from heat and stir in vanilla. Cool over ice, stirring occasionally. Chill until ready to use.

To prepare ahead of time: This can be prepared one day ahead. Be sure to keep it covered and refrigerated.

Note: This can also be flavored with kirsch or other liqueur.

Cakes, Cookies and Pastries

Cakes, Cookies and Pastries

MOTHER'S (DOROTHY WEINER'S) PRUNE TORTE

1 cup shortening
1 cup sugar
2 eggs
3 cups sifted flour
½ teaspoon salt
1 teaspoon baking soda
1 teaspoon lemon juice
1 teaspoon vanilla

for the filling:
12-ounce package pitted
  prunes
⅓ cup raisins
2 green apples, peeled and
  quartered
⅓ cup jam

Make the filling: Put prunes, apples, and raisins through a meat grinder. Place in a bowl, add the jam and mix very thoroughly.

Make the torte: Cream shortening and sugar together. Beat in the eggs. Sift dry ingredients together and add them along with the lemon juice and vanilla. Set aside about ¼ of this dough to use later to make a lattice topping.

Divide the remaining dough into two portions. Grease a 9-inch square pan and pat one portion of the dough into the bottom of the pan. Next place a layer of the filling (use half the amount) on top—then a second layer of the dough—then another layer of the filling. Using the dough that you set aside earlier, cover the filling with a lattice top made with strips of this dough. You may need to work a little more flour into the dough for this purpose. Don't worry too much about the regularity of the strips; they spread during the baking and make a pleasant pattern.

Place torte in a 350° oven and bake 15 minutes; reduce heat to 325° and bake 30 minutes; reduce heat to 300° and bake about 30 to 45 minutes. Remove from oven and cool on a cake rack. When cold wrap in foil and refrigerate at least overnight—several days are even better. Serve cold or at room temperature.

Note: This recipe can be doubled and baked in a larger pan (about 9″ by 18″).

To prepare ahead of time: By all means this can and should be baked several days ahead. If carefully wrapped in foil it will keep for several weeks in the refrigerator—improving with age!

To freeze: Yes, this freezes.

PRINCESS MARGARET ALMOND CAKE [serves about 10]

I first enjoyed this regal cake at the Royal Hotel in Copenhagen; its nobility encouraged this version.

2 ½ cups ground blanched
    almonds (measured
    after grinding)
10 egg whites (1 ¼ cups)
1 cup sugar
¼ teaspoon salt
3 tablespoons maraschino
    liqueur
chopped pistachio nuts
    (for decoration)

fresh strawberries

for the chocolate glaze:
2 tablespoons butter
⅓ cup sugar
2 ounces (squares)
    unsweetened chocolate
¼ cup water
1 teaspoon vanilla

Hint: Use a blender to grind the almonds.

Mix ground almonds and ¾ cup of the sugar in a large bowl. In another bowl beat egg whites with the salt until barely stiff, then gradually beat in the ¼ cup sugar and the maraschino. Grease a ring mold (2 quart) with vegetable shortening and spoon in the batter. Place in a pan of boiling water and bake at 350° for 10 minutes. Reduce heat to 325° and bake about another 20 to 25 minutes. Remove from oven and water bath. Cool about 5 minutes, then invert on a cake rack.

Note: A 1 ½ quart ring mold can also be used but there will be some leftover batter. Use it in small greased cupcake tins or custard cups and bake those as well in a water bath. Or all can be baked in individual pans—if so, reduce baking time somewhat.

Make the chocolate glaze: Combine the butter, sugar, chocolate, and water in a saucepan. Stir over low heat until chocolate melts and mixture is smooth. As soon as this begins to simmer remove from the heat. Add the vanilla.

To finish the cake: Place the cake on a serving dish and spread with the chocolate glaze. Sprinkle with chopped pistachios and surround with fresh strawberries.

To prepare ahead of time: The cake can be baked one or two days ahead of time. I prefer to put the chocolate glaze on the day of the party.

To freeze: The cake can be baked and frozen. Add the chocolate glaze after defrosting.

CHOCOLATE ANGEL FOOD CAKE WITH
CHOCOLATE ICING   [serves 10 to 12]

My way with a chocolate classic.

¾ cup sifted cake flour
¼ cup sugar
¼ cup unsweetened cocoa
  plus 2 tablespoons
10 egg whites (1¼ cups)
½ teaspoon salt
1 teaspoon cream of tartar
1 cup sugar

2 teaspoons vanilla

for the chocolate icing:
  1 6-ounce package semi-sweet
    chocolate chips
  3 tablespoons butter
  ½ cup milk
  sifted powdered sugar

Sift cake flour, ¼ cup sugar, and cocoa together 3 times. Beat egg whites until frothy, then add salt and cream of tartar. Beat until just barely stiff, then gradually beat in the 1 cup sugar and vanilla. Gently fold in the flour-cocoa mixture (don't overmix) and pour or spoon batter into a large angel food cake pan. Bake in a 350° oven for about 45 minutes, or until cake tests done. Remove from oven and turn pan upside down to cool. Do not remove from pan until cake is completely cool. (This cake is easiest to remove if you use a pan with a removable bottom.) If your cake pan doesn't have "legs," place cake upside down over a glass or funnel or something that will keep cake hanging free. After completely cool remove from pan and frost with chocolate icing.

To make the chocolate icing: Melt chocolate chips with the butter and milk over very low heat and stir while it is melting. If possible use a whisk. Remove from heat and cool to room temperature. Add very gradually some sifted powdered sugar and beat thoroughly. Add only enough sugar to aid the icing in keeping its shape. When desired consistency has been achieved, frost the cake.

To prepare ahead of time: This can be baked and frosted the day before serving. Place frosted cake in one of those large plastic cake holders and leave at room temperature. Or—cover cake with plastic wrap and refrigerate, but bring to room temperature before serving.

To freeze: Freeze the cake but add the chocolate icing after defrosting the cake.

DAFFODIL CAKE WITH STRAWBERRY ICING
[serves 12 to 16]

for the white batter:
- 1 ¾ cup egg whites (12 to 14)
- 1 ¼ cups sifted cake flour
- 1 ¾ cups sugar
- ½ teaspoon salt
- 1 ½ teaspoons cream of tartar
- 1 ½ teaspoons vanilla

for the yellow batter:
- 5 egg yolks
- 2 tablespoons cake flour
- 2 tablespoons sugar
- 1 tablespoon grated orange rind

for the strawberry icing:
- ¼ cup softened butter
- 1 pound powdered sugar
- ⅔ cup mashed fresh strawberries

White batter: Sift flour with ¾ cup of the sugar, then sift again about 3 times. Beat egg whites with the salt and cream of tartar until soft peaks are formed, then gradually beat in the remaining 1 cup sugar about ¼ cup at a time. Fold in the vanilla. Sift flour mixture over egg whites—about ¼ at a time—and fold in gently. Place ⅓ of this white batter in a separate bowl.

164

Yellow batter: Beat egg yolks with the flour and sugar until very thick. Fold in grated orange rind. Fold this yellow batter into the white batter that you placed in a separate bowl.

To bake cake: Spoon the two batters alternately into an ungreased 10-inch angel food cake pan, ending with white batter on the top. With a spatula or knife cut through the batter twice. Smooth top of cake batter. Bake on the lower rack of the oven at 375° for 35 to 40 minutes—or until a toothpick inserted in center comes out clean. Invert pan over the neck of a bottle. Let cake cool completely— about 2 hours.

To make strawberry icing: Beat butter and sugar together, then gradually beat in strawberries until desired consistency is obtained. Frost the cooled cake.

To prepare ahead of time: The cake can be baked the day before. I prefer to add the strawberry icing the day I plan to serve the cake.

To freeze: The cake can be frozen but add the strawberry icing after defrosting.

LEMON CHIFFON CAKE WITH LEMON ICING

[serves 12 to 16]

2 ¼ cups sifted cake flour
1 ½ cups sugar
3 teaspoons baking powder
1 teaspoon salt
½ cup salad oil
5 egg yolks
¾ cup cold water
2 teaspoons vanilla
grated rind of 1 lemon
8 egg whites

½ teaspoon cream of tartar

for the lemon icing:
2 teaspoons soft butter
grated rind of 1 lemon
juice of 1 lemon
1 pound powdered sugar
milk or water (only if
    needed)

Sift dry ingredients (cake flour, sugar, baking powder, and salt) together several times, then place in a large mixing bowl. Add the oil, egg yolks, water, vanilla, and lemon rind and beat until smooth.

Place egg whites and cream of tartar in a separate bowl and whip until whites are very stiff. Pour egg yolk mixture gradually over the

165

beaten whites and carefully fold into the whites. Pour batter into a large angel food pan—ungreased—and bake for 55 minutes in a 325° oven. Increase temperature to 350° and bake about another 15 minutes. Remove from oven and turn upside down—placing tube part over the neck of a bottle to cool. After cake is completely cold (about 2 hours) remove from pan.

To make the lemon icing: Combine butter, lemon rind, lemon juice, and powdered sugar. Beat thoroughly, adding a little milk or water only if necessary to obtain desired consistency. Frost the cake.

Note: This is a deliciously light cake to serve with fresh raspberries or strawberries.

To prepare ahead of time: This cake can be baked and frosted the day before. Place in one of those large plastic cake holders and leave at room temperature. Or—cover cake with plastic wrap and refrigerate, but bring to room temperature before serving.

To freeze: The cake can be frozen. I recommend adding the lemon icing after defrosting.

JELLY ROLL WITH DICED SUGARED ALMONDS
[serves 8 to 10]

It is the topping on this jelly roll that makes it extraordinary. The idea for this embellishment came from my observation of same at the Cordon Bleu Cooking School in Paris.

4 eggs (room temperature)	3 tablespoons butter,
1 cup sugar	melted and cooled
1 cup sifted cake flour	1 cup currant jelly
1 teaspoon baking powder	¼ cup finely diced almonds
¼ teaspoon salt	1 tablespoon sugar
1 teaspoon vanilla	

Grease a shallow baking pan (11″ by 17″) and line with waxed paper. Grease waxed paper heavily too. Sift flour, baking powder, and salt together 3 times and leave in the sifter. Beat eggs until light, then gradually beat in the 1 cup of sugar, continuing to beat until very thick (about 8 to 10 minutes with an electric mixer). Add the vanilla. Sift and fold in the dry ingredients. Pour and cut in the cooled butter—then fold in with a few quick strokes. Pour into prepared pan and bake at 350° for 15 to 20 minutes. Remove from oven and immediately turn upside down on a damp towel. Carefully remove waxed paper. Cut off crisp edges. Spread roll with about ¾ cup of the currant jelly and roll up. Place damp towel over it for a few minutes, then transfer to a serving platter and let cool.

Prepare sugared almonds: Spread diced almonds on a baking pan. Sprinkle them with the 1 tablespoon sugar. Place under a broiling unit and toast, stirring very frequently, and watching every moment so they don't burn. Warning: Do not attempt to do anything else while you are preparing these almonds. As soon as they are glazed and toasted remove from oven.

To finish the jelly roll: Spread the top of the jelly roll with the remaining currant jolly, then sprinkle with the diced sugared almonds. Cut in diagonal slices and serve.

To prepare ahead of time: The jelly roll can be baked and rolled the day before. Add the topping the day you plan to serve it.

To freeze: The jelly roll can be frozen but do so without the topping. Add that the day you plan to serve it.

MODERN FRUIT CAKE CHEZ MELLINKOFF

[serves many]

2 cups seedless raisins	2 cups sugar
1½ cups candied cherries (leave these whole)	7 eggs, extra large
	2 teaspoons vanilla
1½ cups sliced dates (use a scissors to speed this task)	3½ cups sifted flour
	1 teaspoon salt
	1 teaspoon baking powder
2 cups butter (1 pound) at room temperature	½ teaspoon cream of tartar

Rinse raisins with very hot water, drain thoroughly, then dry on paper towels.

Combine raisins, sliced dates, and cherries in one large bowl. Sift 2 cups of the flour over them and toss thoroughly to coat the fruit. (I use my hands for this job.)

Cream butter with the sugar until light and fluffy. Beat in the eggs one at a time. Add vanilla and beat again. Continue beating until very fluffy. Sift remaining flour with the salt, baking powder, and cream of tartar. Add to egg mixture and stir until thoroughly incorporated. Fold this into the floured fruit mixture and stir until all is thoroughly combined. Spoon batter into a well greased and floured tube cake pan (that holds 3½ to 4 quarts) and bake at 300° for about 2 hours. Remove from oven, wait a few minutes, then remove from pan and finish cooling on a cake rack.

Note: If you prefer this can be baked in two smaller tube pans—reduce the length of baking time. You will have to judge this yourself depending on the size and shape of your pans. Test occasionally with a toothpick.

To prepare ahead of time: This can be prepared several weeks ahead of time. Keep it well wrapped in a double thickness of foil in the refrigerator. Bring to room temperature before serving.

To freeze: This freezes beautifully. Defrost completely and bring to room temperature before serving.

LANE CAKE   [serves 24 or more]

This is my variation of an old-time southern favorite; its remarkable fruit-nut filling makes it an ideal cake for fall and winter festive occasions.

1 cup butter	*for the filling:*
2¼ cups sugar	12 egg yolks
2 teaspoons vanilla	1¾ cups sugar
3¼ cups sifted cake flour	½ teaspoon salt
3½ teaspoons baking powder	¾ cup butter
1 teaspoon salt	¾ cup bourbon whiskey
1¼ cups milk	1⅔ cups coarsely chopped
8 egg whites	pecans
	1½ cups raisins, chopped
	1⅔ cups candied cherries
	1⅔ cups shredded coconut

Cream butter, 1½ cups of the sugar, and vanilla until light and fluffy. Sift flour, baking powder, and salt together 2 or 3 times. Add alternately with the milk, mixing after each addition—but do not overbeat. Beat egg whites in a separate bowl until they form soft peaks, then gradually beat in the remaining ¾ cup of sugar. Fold whites into the first mixture then spoon the batter into 3 greased and floured 10-inch layer cake pans. Bake at 350° for about 25 to 30 minutes or until cakes test done. Cool for 5 minutes, then remove from pans. Finish cooling on cake racks.

To prepare filling: Place egg yolks in the top of a double boiler and beat slightly. Add sugar, salt, and butter. Cook over simmering water, stirring, until mixture has thickened. Remove from heat and add the bourbon. Beat for about 1 minute. Stir in the pecans, raisins, cherries, and coconut.

To assemble the cake: Spread the filling on the layers and stack them. Cover top and sides with remaining filling. Let cake stand for an hour, then spread any filling that has dripped off back on the top and sides of cake. Repeat again later if necessary.

To prepare ahead of time: This cake is best if prepared several days ahead (or several weeks). Keep well wrapped and refrigerated. Bring to room temperature before serving.

To freeze: Yes, this can be frozen. Wrap first in plastic wrap, then with heavy foil. Defrost and bring to room temperature before serving.

TINY CHOCOLATE SLICES WITH RASPBERRY JAM AND CHOCOLATE ICING   [makes about 3 dozen very tiny squares]

These are very rich and delicate. Serve them in tiny paper cups—or cut them larger, then serve on dessert plates with forks.

½ cup butter
½ cup sugar
4 ounces (4 squares) semi-
    sweet chocolate
4 eggs
½ teaspoon vanilla
pinch of salt

seedless raspberry jam

for the chocolate icing:
4 ounces dark sweet
    chocolate
⅓ cup heavy whipping
    cream

Prepare the chocolate slices: Melt chocolate and cool slightly Cream butter and sugar, then beat in eggs, vanilla, and salt. Beat in melted chocolate. Bake in a greased and floured pan (I use one that is 10½" by 15" by ½") at 325° for 25 minutes (about). Remove from oven (but not from pan). Cool.

Make the chocolate icing: Melt chocolate, heat cream, then whip with a whisk until combined and cool and of spreading consistency.

To assemble: Cut the baked chocolate layer in long strips about 1½ inches wide. Cover half the strips with a thin layer of seedless raspberry jam. Top with remaining strips. Frost with the chocolate icing. (If you have icing left over it will keep in the refrigerator for several weeks—or—freeze it.) Cut strips into tiny slices or squares.

To prepare ahead of time: These can be made the day before. Store (well covered) in the refrigerator.

To freeze: These can be frozen.

VERY DARK CHOCOLATE CRISPS [makes about 2 dozen]

3 egg whites
¾ cup sugar
1 teaspoon vanilla

2 ounces (squares) unsweetened chocolate, melted

Beat egg whites until stiff. Gradually beat in sugar and add vanilla. Add melted chocolate and continue to beat until mixture suddenly loses its volume. This is what you want—don't worry—it is supposed to go "flat." Pour batter into an 11" by 17" greased and floured pan. Bake at 275° for about 40 to 50 minutes or until very crisp to the touch. Remove from oven and cool 1 minute. Using a sharp knife cut in squares and remove from pan.

To prepare ahead of time: These can be baked several days ahead. Store between layers of waxed paper in an airtight tin.

To freeze: Yes, these can be frozen.

ALMOND LACE CHOCOLATE SANDWICHES

[makes about 1 dozen
or more "sandwiches"]

1 scant cup blanched almonds	2 tablespoons milk
½ cup butter	*chocolate icing*
½ cup sugar	(use recipe on p. 169)
1 tablespoon plus 2 teaspoons flour	

Grind almonds in a blender. Melt butter in a heavy saucepan over low heat. Add sugar, flour, and milk and stir until well combined. Add ground almonds. Cook until bubbly, stirring frequently to keep it from burning, for about 1 minute. Cool.

Drop teaspoonfuls of this almond mixture (leaving about 4 inches between each to allow for spreading) on greased and floured cookie sheets. Bake at 350° for approximately 5 to 7 minutes or until cookies are medium brown in color. Don't try baking too many at one time. Watch that they brown well but do not burn. Remove from oven, let stand about 1 minute, then remove quickly with the aid of a spatula and place on waxed paper. If cookies become too crisp to remove from pan return to oven briefly, then try again.

To make sandwiches: Spread half the cookies with the prepared chocolate icing, then top with the others. These are best if the sandwiches are made not more than several hours before serving.

Note: These cookies are equally delectable eaten without any filling. You might also like to try them filled with whipped cream or ice cream and served as a dessert with fresh strawberries.

To prepare ahead of time: These cookies can be baked (but not filled) several days ahead. Pack them carefully between layers of waxed paper in airtight tins.

To freeze: These cookies can be frozen (unfilled). Pack them carefully in a large airtight tin between layers of waxed paper or plastic wrap.

COCONUT-TOPPED CHOCOLATE CHIP BROWNIES

[makes 16 to 24]

4 ounces dark sweet
   chocolate
⅓ cup butter
½ cup chocolate chips
⅔ cup sifted flour
½ teaspoon baking powder
¼ teaspoon salt
2 eggs
½ cup sugar
1 teaspoon vanilla

for the topping:
1 ⅓ cups angel flake
   grated coconut (comes
   in cans)
¼ cup brown sugar (packed
   for measuring)
½ cup chopped walnuts
2 tablespoons cream

Prepare the topping first: Combine all the ingredients and mix thoroughly with a fork—or use your hands. Set aside.

Melt chocolate and butter over low heat and cool. Sift flour, baking powder, and salt together. Beat eggs and then gradually beat in sugar and vanilla. Add melted chocolate-butter mixture. Stir in sifted dry ingredients until combined but do not overmix. Stir in chocolate chips. Spread this batter in a greased and floured 8- or 9-inch square pan. Sprinkle the prepared topping over the batter. Bake at 350° for about 30 minutes or longer. Time will depend somewhat on size of pan. Remove from oven and cool, then cut in squares.

To prepare ahead of time: These can be baked the day before. Pack squares between layers of waxed paper in an airtight tin. Refrigerate but bring to room temperature before serving.

To freeze: Yes, these can be frozen.

FRUIT-SPICE BARS

[makes about 3 dozen]

½ cup soft butter
1 ¼ cups brown sugar
   (pack to measure)
1 egg
½ cup honey
2 cups sifted flour
1 teaspoon baking powder
1 teaspoon salt
1 teaspoon cinnamon
½ teaspoon nutmeg

¼ teaspoon cloves
¼ teaspoon baking soda
¾ cup sliced candied
   cherries
¾ cup sliced dates
1 cup chopped nuts
for the glaze:
1 cup sifted powdered sugar
1 teaspoon vanilla
water

Cream butter and sugar together until fluffy. Add egg and honey and beat. Sift all dry ingredients together several times. Sprinkle ½ cup of the dry ingredients over the cherries, dates, and nuts and coat well. Add dry ingredients to batter and stir until blended. Do the same with the coated fruit mixture.

Spread batter in a greased and floured pan (about 9" by 13") and bake at 350° for about 25 to 30 minutes. Cool in the pan on a cake rack.

Prepare the glaze: Add vanilla to the sifted powdered sugar along with small spoonfuls of water until glaze is of spreading consistency. Frost the cookies, then cut in bars and serve.

To prepare ahead of time: These can be baked several days ahead. Pack between layers of waxed paper in airtight tins.

To freeze: These bars can be frozen.

DATE AND WALNUT BARS [makes 2 to 3 dozen]

½ cup soft butter
1 cup sugar
2 eggs
¾ cup sifted flour
¼ teaspoon baking powder
¼ teaspoon salt

1 teaspoon vanilla
1 cup chopped walnuts
1½ cups sliced dates
  (about 8 ounces of
  pitted dates)
some sifted powdered sugar

Cream butter and sugar together. Beat in eggs. Sift dry ingredients together and add along with the vanilla. Stir in walnuts and dates. Spread batter in a greased and floured pan (9" by 13") and bake at 350° for 20 to 25 minutes. Cool in the pan on a rack, then cut into bars. Sprinkle with powdered sugar.

To prepare ahead of time: These can be baked several days ahead. Keep between layers of waxed paper in airtight tins.

To freeze: These can be frozen.

STUFFED DATES BAKED   [makes about 4 dozen]

4 dozen pitted dates (about)   1 ¼ cups sifted flour
walnut halves   ½ teaspoon salt
¼ cup butter   ¼ teaspoon baking powder
¾ cup brown sugar (pack   ½ teaspoon baking soda
   to measure)   ½ cup sour cream
1 egg   *vanilla icing*
1 teaspoon vanilla   (see recipe below)

Stuff each date with a walnut half. Break nuts in pieces if necessary but be sure to use the entire walnut half in each date. Set aside.

Cream butter and sugar until fluffy. Beat in egg and vanilla. Sift dry ingredients together, then add them alternately with the sour cream.

Dip each stuffed date in the prepared batter, covering all sides. Place on greased cookie sheets. Bake at 400° for about 8 to 12 minutes. Watch that they don't burn.

Vanilla icing:
   Note: This is optional. The cookies are quite delicious without the icing.

¼ cup melted butter   1 teaspoon vanilla
1 cup sifted powdered sugar   a little milk

Combine butter, sugar, and vanilla. Add powdered sugar. Add milk a very little at a time until an icing of spreading consistency is obtained. Frost the cookies.

To prepare ahead of time: These can be baked several days ahead. Do not frost until you plan to serve them.

To freeze: These can be baked and frozen. Ice them only after they have been defrosted and before you plan to serve them.

OLD FASHIONED FILLED RAISIN COOKIES

[makes about 2 dozen or more]

½ cup butter or vegetable
  shortening
1 cup sugar
1 egg
1 teaspoon vanilla
3½ cups sifted flour
1 teaspoon baking powder

½ teaspoon salt
½ cup milk
for the filling:
1 cup raisins
1 tablespoon flour
¾ cup sugar
¾ cup boiling water

Cream butter and sugar together. Beat in egg and vanilla. Sift dry ingredients together, then add alternately with the milk. Chill.

Combine ingredients for the filling. Cook, stirring, until thickened. Cool, then chill.

Roll out cookie dough to about ⅛ inch thickness. Cut in 2½-inch rounds. Put a teaspoon of filling on half the rounds, then top with the others. Press edges together. Prick tops once with a fork. Bake at 375° for 10 to 15 minutes.

To prepare ahead of time: These can be baked several days ahead. Store between layers of waxed paper in airtight tins.

To freeze: These can be frozen.

HAZELNUT (FILBERT) KISSES

[makes 3 dozen or more]

3 cups hazelnuts (filberts)
1⅓ cups sugar

4 egg whites

Toast nuts in a 350° oven until lightly browned. Remove and rub off outer skins. (Don't worry if some of the brown outer skin remains.) Grind nuts in a blender.

Beat egg whites until stiff but not dry. Gradualy beat in the sugar. Fold in the ground nuts and drop from a teaspoon on greased and floured baking pans. Bake at 250° for 45 minutes to an hour.

To prepare ahead of time: These can be baked several days ahead. Pack between layers of waxed paper in airtight tins.

To freeze: These can be frozen.

WALNUT WHOLE EGG MACAROONS

[makes about 3 dozen or more]

¾ pound walnuts, ground
1½ cups sugar

1 teaspoon vanilla
3 eggs, slightly beaten

Combine all the ingredients and mix until well combined. Drop by teaspoonfuls on greased and floured cookie sheets. Bake at 325° to 350° until firm and lightly browned—about 15 to 20 minutes.

To prepare ahead of time: These can be baked several days ahead. Pack in airtight tins between layers of waxed paper.

To freeze: These can be frozen.

ALMOND MACAROONS WITH PIÑON NUTS

[makes 2 to 3 dozen]

8 ounces almond paste
1 cup sugar

3 large egg whites
piñon nuts

Cut up almond paste, add sugar and 1 egg white and beat until crumbly. Add remaining egg whites and beat slowly with an electric mixer until smooth. Place mixture in a pastry bag with a no. 6 round tube and drop on baking pans that have been greased and floured (or use silicone non-sticking baking paper). Make the macaroons about ¾ inch in diameter. If you lack a pastry bag, just drop the mixture by teaspoonfuls. Top each macaroon with 6 to 10 piñon nuts. Bake at 325° for about 20 to 30 minutes. Remove from oven and loosen with a spatula at once.

To prepare ahead of time: These can be baked a day or two ahead. Keep in airtight tins between layers of waxed paper.

To freeze: These freeze beautifully.

CHOCOLATE MACAROONS

[makes 2 to 3 dozen]

8 ounces almond paste
1 cup sugar
3 egg whites

1 ounce (1 square) unsweetened chocolate, melted
and cooled

Beat almond paste with the sugar. Add one egg white and beat again. Gradually add remaining egg whites and beat until combined. Stir in melted chocolate.

Drop by teaspoonfuls on greased and floured baking sheets. (Or you can use a pastry bag with a no. 6 round tube.) Macaroons should be about ¾ inch in diameter. Bake at 325° for about 20 to 30 minutes.

To prepare ahead of time: These can be baked a day or two ahead. Keep in airtight tins between layers of waxed paper.

To freeze: Yes, you can freeze these.

RICH PASTRY   [enough for one 10-inch pie, top
                                and bottom, or two 10-inch shells]

2 ¼ cups sifted flour   1 egg
½ teaspoon salt   2 tablespoons lemon juice
¾ cup shortening   2 tablespoons ice water
   (can use part butter)

Note: All butter can be used; my preference is half butter and half vegetable shortening. The lemon juice can be eliminated, if so, replace with 2 additional tablespoons of ice water.

Mix flour and salt together, then cut in the shortening. Combine egg, lemon juice, and ice water and beat slightly. Pour over the flour-shortening and cut in with a knife until all of the dry ingredients are absorbed. Turn out and knead gently about 2 or 3 times. Chill at least 1 hour—overnight is better. The pastry can be cut in half and chilled in two portions ready to roll out.

To prepare ahead of time: This can be prepared several days ahead. Keep well wrapped in the refrigerator.

To freeze: Yes, this freezes.

CREAM CHEESE-BUTTER PASTRY [enough for one 10-inch pie, top and bottom, or two 10-inch shells]

1 cup butter (½ pound)	2 cups sifted flour
8 ounces cream cheese	¼ teaspoon salt

Cream butter and cheese. Combine flour and salt and add, blending it with a fork or a pastry blender or your fingers—gradually forming pastry into a ball. Divide in desired portions, flatten, wrap, and chill for at least 1 hour—longer is better.

To prepare ahead of time: This can be made 2 or 3 days ahead. Keep well wrapped in the refrigerator.

To freeze: Yes, this freezes.

HOT BANANA PASTRIES WITH KIRSCH CREAM

A candid imitation of the superb pastries I ate again and again at the Auberge Rennequin in Paris.

Baked puff pastry rounds (one per person)	sugar
	kirsch
thinly sliced bananas (⅓ to ½ banana per person)	heavy cream, whipped, lightly sweetened and flavored with kirsch

To make puff pastry rounds: Use the recipe for puff pastry on p. 152 or buy some. Puff pastry trimmings are fine for this too. The amount needed will depend on how many you plan to serve.

Roll pastry very thin (about ⅛ inch thick). Cut in 5-inch circles (they will shrink slightly when baked). Place them on ungreased baking pans. Chill in refrigerator or freezer. Bake at 425° for about 15 minutes. Reduce heat to 375° or 350° and bake until well browned and thoroughly cooked through. Watch that they do not burn.

To finish: Shortly before serving reheat baked pastry rounds in a 300° oven for about 10 minutes. You can do this while you are clearing the table of the main course or salad course—if you serve the latter last. Do not overheat or overbake. Remove from oven.

Turn on your broiling unit. Now cover each pastry round with overlapping slices of banana—be generous and cover every part of the pastry possible. Sprinkle the sliced bananas with sugar. Place under broiling unit and now be sure to WATCH. Grill only long enough to melt and partly caramelize the sugar. Remove from oven and quickly (with spatula) place on individual dessert plates. Sprinkle tops of each with a half teaspoon of kirsch. Serve at once. Pass kirsch flavored whipped cream separately.

Note: Unless you have expert help in the kitchen don't try serving these to too many guests—about six to eight is maximum if you are doing this yourself.

To prepare ahead of time: The puff pastry rounds can be baked the day before or in the morning. Then proceed with the recipe as directed.

To freeze: The puff pastry rounds can be frozen in their unbaked state. As a matter of fact it is nice to have some on hand for emergencies.

WALNUT BOATS WITH COFFEE ICING
[makes 2 to 3 dozen depending on size of barquette molds]

Inspired in part by some exquisite walnut tartlets I sampled in Amsterdam.

1 recipe of rich pastry
    (on p. 177)
for the walnut filling:
  ½ cup soft butter
  ⅔ cup sugar
  2 eggs
  1 teaspoon vanilla
  2 cups walnuts, measured
    then ground in a
    blender
  ⅛ teaspoon salt

for the coffee icing:
  1 pound powdered sugar
  2 tablespoons melted butter
  ⅓ cup boiling water
  6 level teaspoons powered
    coffee

walnut halves (for decoration)

Make the walnut filling: Cream butter and sugar. Beat in eggs and vanilla. Stir in ground walnuts and salt.

To make the boats: Line barquette (boat-shaped) molds with pastry (rolled about ⅛ inch thick). Fill about ¾ full with the walnut mixture. Bake at 425° to 450° for 10 to 15 minutes. Remove and cool on racks.

Make the coffee icing: Dissolve powdered coffee in boiling water. Place sugar in a large bowl. Gradually beat in the butter and dissolved coffee until a spreading consistency is obtained. I find it easiest to do this with an electric mixer. This is more than you need but the extra will keep for weeks in the refrigerator—longer in the freezer. Stir before using. Of course you can make half a recipe if you prefer.

To finish the walnut boats: Frost with the coffee icing and top each one with a walnut half.

To prepare ahead of time: The pastry can be made and refrigerated several days ahead as can the coffee icing. Stir icing before using.

To freeze: The baked walnut boats freeze beautifully—but do so without icing. My method is this: I defrost the coffee icing. Then I defrost the boats; I heat them for 3 to 5 minutes in a 325° oven just to crisp the pastry and then cool them. I stir the coffee icing, then I finish the frosting, etc.

PISTACHIO TARTLETS (REAL!)

[makes 2 to 3 dozen very small ones]

No mockery these, but the real thing—once bitten into a gorgeous green color emerges, and without any artificial food coloring.

rich pastry (half a recipe on p. 177)
1¼ cups blanched pistachios (see directions below)

⅔ cup sugar
grated rind of 1 large lemon
4 egg whites
pinch of salt

To blanch pistachios: Place pistachios in boiling water and simmer for five minutes. Drain and rub them on paper towels to help remove skins. Finish the job by hand—much work, but worth it.

Whirl nuts in the blender about ⅓ at a time. If you like, reserve about ¼ cup of the nuts for decoration. Combine ground nuts with ⅓ cup of the sugar and the grated lemon rind. Beat egg whites with the salt until barely stiff then gradually beat in remaining sugar. Fold whites into nut mixture.

Roll pastry thin and cut in small circles to fit your tartlet pans—or lacking those, some small muffin tins. Fill pastry lined tins about ¾ full with the pistachio mixture. Top each (if desired) with a few whole pistachio nuts. Bake at 375° for 20 to 30 minutes or until pastry is well browned. Remove from pans at once and cool on racks.

To prepare ahead of time: These can be baked the day before. As soon as they are cool pack them between layers of waxed paper in airtight tins.

To freeze: These can be frozen. Defrost, then to crisp the pastry place in a 325° oven for 3 to 5 minutes. Cool again and then serve.

GINGER-WALNUT TARTLETS
[makes 18 to 24 very small round tartlets]

Candied ginger or preserved ginger appeared in a great variety of pastries and desserts that we ate in Amsterdam; they stimulated this creation.

rich pastry (½ recipe
    on p. 177)
paper-thin slices of
    preserved ginger
¼ cup soft butter
⅓ cup sugar
1 egg

1 teaspoon vanilla
1 cup walnuts, measured then
    ground in a blender
⅛ teaspoon salt
¼ cup chopped preserved
    ginger

Cream butter with sugar, then beat in eggs and vanilla. Stir in walnuts, salt, and chopped ginger.

Line small round pans (English "patty" pans are perfect for this) with pastry that has been rolled about ⅛ inch thick. Fill ½ full with walnut mixture. Top each with a thin slice of preserved ginger. Bake at 425° or 450° for 10 to 15 minutes. Remove and cool on racks.

To prepare ahead of time: These can be baked the day before. After they are cool pack them in airtight tins between layers of waxed paper.

To freeze: These do freeze. To use: defrost, then crisp pastry in a 325° oven for 3 to 5 minutes. Remove and cool again, then serve.

APPLE, RAISIN, AND PIÑON NUT TARTS
[makes about 24 or more medium-size tarts]

In the manner of some delicate and unusual apple tarts we enjoyed at the Villa d'Este on Lake Como.

double recipe of rich pastry
(on p. 177)
9 large green apples (about
9 cups thinly sliced
apples)
1¾ cups sugar
4½ tablespoons flour
¾ teaspoon salt

¼ teaspoon nutmeg
1½ teaspoons cinnamon
5 tablespoons butter
1 tablespoon lemon juice
½ cup raisins, rinsed in hot
water, then drained and
dried on paper towels
¾ cup toasted piñon nuts

Combine apples, sugar, flour, salt, nutmeg, cinnamon, butter, lemon juice, and raisins and place in a large skillet or large pot. Cook over moderate heat, stirring, until apples are almost but not quite cooked. Remove from heat and stir in toasted piñon nuts. Set aside.

Line medium-size tart pans (or use regular size metal muffin pans) with rich pastry. Spoon in apple filling. Decorate the top of each with a pastry strip lattice cover. Bake at 425° for about 20 to 25 minutes or until pastry is well browned and apples are cooked. Do not overbake.

Remove from oven and now comes the important task of removing the tarts from the pans. While tarts are still hot—using hot pad holders, etc.—carefully remove from pans and place them right side up on greased cake racks. This must be done while the pastry is still hot or the sugar that has weeped over the edge will stick and make it virtually impossible to loosen. Be sure to loosen pastry from edges of pans with a tiny sharp knife before trying to remove. This is not a difficult procedure—just takes patience and a little practice.

To serve: These can be served either at room temperature or hot. To reheat, place tarts on baking pans and heat in a 350° oven but do not overcook.

To prepare ahead of time: These can be baked the day before. Cover and refrigerate. Reheat before serving.

To freeze: These are absolutely ideal freezer items. Defrost, then reheat in a 350° oven.

BANANA CREAM PIE IN A COCONUT CRUST

[serves 6 to 8]

2 cups angel flake coconut
　(about 2 cans)
⅓ cup melted butter
for the filling:

3 tablespoons flour	2 tablespoons butter
3 tablespoons cornstarch	5 egg yolks
¼ teaspoon salt	1½ teaspoons vanilla
½ cup sugar (scant)	2 large bananas
1 cup milk	whipped cream for decorating
1½ cups light cream	(optional)

Make the crust: Combine coconut and butter in a bowl and mix. Press into a buttered 10-inch pie pan. Bake at 300° for about 30 minutes or more—until nicely toasted. Remove from oven and cool.

Make the filling: Combine flour, cornstarch, salt, and sugar in the top of a double boiler. Mix thoroughly, then stir in the milk, cream, and butter. Cook, stirring, over simmering water until thick. Beat egg yolks in a separate bowl, then gradually beat in the hot mixture. Return to the double boiler and cook, stirring constantly, until very thick. Remove from heat and add vanilla. Cool over ice, stirring occasionally. Chill.

To assemble: Slice one banana in bottom of coconut crust. Add some custard, then another banana and the remaining custard. Decorate with whipped cream and chill until time to serve.

To prepare ahead of time: The crust and the custard can be prepared the day before. Keep each covered and refrigerated. Assemble pie the day you plan to serve.

To freeze: The coconut crust will freeze.

OPEN FACE PEACH PIE [serves 6 to 8]

cream cheese-butter pastry
    (½ recipe on p. 178)
1 cup brown sugar (pack
    to measeure)
¼ cup sugar
¼ teaspoon salt

1 teaspoon nutmeg
½ cup flour
6 or 7 fresh peaches, peeled,
    then cut in eighths
4 tablespoons butter

Line a 10-inch pie dish with the pastry and chill. Combine the two kinds of sugar, salt, nutmeg, and flour and mix thoroughly. Place ¾ cup of this mixture in the bottom of chilled pastry shell. Place sliced peaches on top. Mix butter with the remaining sugar-flour mixture and sprinkle on top of peaches. Bake at 400° for 40 to 50 minutes.

To prepare ahead of time: This can be baked the day before. Keep covered and refrigerated. Reheat before serving—or—serve cold.

To freeze: This can be frozen. Defrost, then reheat before serving.

COCONUT CREAM PIE [serves 6 to 8]

one 10-inch baked pie shell
    (use ½ recipe of rich
    pastry on p. 177)
¾ cup sugar
3 tablespoons cornstarch
3 tablespoons flour
¼ teaspoon salt
2½ cups milk
¼ cup butter

5 egg yolks
1 teaspoon vanilla
2 cups grated coconut (canned
    is fine for this)
5 egg whites
⅛ teaspoon cream of tartar
¼ teaspoon salt
10 tablespoons sugar

Mix sugar, cornstarch, flour, and salt in the top of a double boiler, then stir in the milk and butter. Cook and stir until thick. Beat egg yolks in a separate bowl and gradually add hot mixture beating at the same time. Return to double boiler and cook until very thick, stirring constantly. Remove from heat and cool over ice, stirring occasionally. Add vanilla and chill.

Add 1 cup of the coconut to chilled custard and spoon into baked pastry shell. Beat egg whites with the salt and cream of tartar until barely stiff, then gradually beat in the 10 tablespoons of sugar, beating until very stiff and glossy. Spread this in peaks on top of the custard, covering it completely. Sprinkle the remaining 1 cup of coconut on the meringue. Bake in a 350° oven for 15 to 20 minutes, or until meringue and coconut are well browned. Cool on a cake rack, then chill. Serve very cold.

To prepare ahead of time: The pastry shell and the custard can be prepared the day before. Keep refrigerated. Assemble and add the meringue the day you plan to serve the pie.

To freeze: The pastry shell can be baked and frozen. Defrost, then heat briefly in a moderate oven to crisp.

LAYERED PUMPKIN-MINCE PIE [serves 6 to 8]

pastry for one 10-inch shell
(use ½ recipe of either
rich pastry on p. 177 or
cream cheese pastry
on p. 178)
1 quart of mincemeat
2 or 3 tablespoons brandy

for the pumpkin filling:
2 cups canned pumpkin
1 ⅔ cups evaporated milk
3 eggs
¾ cup sugar
½ teaspoon salt
1 tablespoon flour
1 ¼ teaspoons cinnamon
½ teaspoon nutmeg
1 teaspon ginger
¼ teaspoon cloves
¼ teaspoon allspice

Roll out pastry and fit into pie dish. You will need a deep 10-inch dish. (I use a white porcelain French quiche dish.) Chill.

Combine mincemeat with brandy and set aside.

Beat pumpkin, evaporated milk, and eggs together. Mix sugar, salt, flour, and spices together in a separate bowl, then beat into the pumpkin mixture.

Spoon mincemeat into pie shell. Add the pumpkin filling spooning carefully on top of mincemeat. (If there is too much pumpkin filling bake the extra in a few greased custard cups.)

Place filled pastry shell in a 425° oven for 20 minutes. Reduce heat to 325° and bake about 30 minutes longer. If a knife inserted in the custard comes out clean it is done. Remove and cool on a rack. Serve at room temperature.

To prepare ahead of time: Pastry can be made several days ahead and refrigerated. The pie is at its best baked and eaten the same day.

To freeze: The pastry, of course, can be frozen. The pie itself is not at its best after freezing. Don't hesitate, however, to freeze leftovers —it still makes for good family fare.

Desserts

Desserts

JARDIN DES DÉLICES [serves few or many]

A garden of delightful temptations—without the Fall.

miniature babas au rhum
(recipe on p. 191)
tiny vanilla ice cream balls—
if possible use the large
end of a melon ball
scooper
Chocolate sauce
(see recipe below)
Raspberry purée
(see recipe below)
fresh raspberries

other fruits of the season:
fresh strawberries
fresh pineapple, sliced
cantaloupe balls
watermelon balls
peaches, peeled and quartered
plums, peeled and halved
apricots, halved

Chocolate sauce:
8 ounces dark sweet
chocolate
1 cup heavy cream (or more
depending on how thin
you want the sauce)

rum or brandy to taste

Combine chocolate and cream and melt over very low heat, stirring.
Add rum or brandy. Serve hot or cold.

Raspberry purée:
frozen raspberries
sugar to taste

framboise liqueur to taste

Defrost raspberries. Whirl in a blender, then put raspberries through
a sieve and eliminate the seeds. Sweeten and flavor to taste. Serve
cold.

To assemble: Arrange the "jardin" either on several large platters or a buffet cart or side table. The amount of space needed will depend on how many guests you are serving. Items should be arranged something like this:

1. miniature babas au rhum on a flat serving dish—
2. tiny ice cream balls in a bowl—
3. chocolate sauce in a bowl next to ice cream—
4. fresh raspberries in a bowl or on a dish—
5. raspberry purée in a bowl next to the fresh raspberries—
6. other fruits of the season arranged in separate "bouquets" either on dishes or platters. If only a relatively few guests are to be served this can all be arranged in tiny "bouquets" on one dish.

To serve: It is desirable to serve this to your guests yourself or to explain how they should serve themselves. Each individual's dessert plate should be filled in this way:

1. one miniature baba au rhum—
2. one tiny ice cream ball with a small spoonful of chocolate sauce over it—
3. a good spoonful of fresh raspberries with some of the raspberry purée spooned over them—
4. a sampling of the other fruits arranged in miniature "bouquets" on the plate.

Hint: Use large dinner plates for this dessert so that all the lovely items can be kept quite separate.

To prepare ahead of time: The babas can be baked one or two days ahead, then dipped in syrup the morning of the party. The chocolate sauce can be made several days ahead.

To freeze: Babas freeze (see recipe on p. 191). Chocolate sauce can be frozen and of course, the ice cream balls should be scooped, covered well, and kept frozen until time to serve.

BABA AU RHUM [makes about 12 regular size babas]

¼ cup warm water
1 package dry yeast
1 teaspoon sugar
½ cup sifted flour
¼ cup milk
4 eggs
2 cups sifted flour
1 teaspoon salt
2 tablespoons sugar
¼ cup soft butter
½ teaspoon lemon extract
1 teaspoon vanilla

for the rum syrup:

4 cups water
2 cups sugar
1 lemon
1 orange
⅔ cup dark Jamaican rum

strained apricot jam, slightly
heated, or some melted jelly

Dissolve yeast in the water, then stir in the 1 teaspoon of sugar, the ¼ cup of milk, and the ½ cup sifted flour. Set aside while you do the rest of the mixing.

Put eggs, the 2 cups of flour, salt, and sugar in a large bowl and beat vigorously either with a wooden spoon or with an electric dough hook. Add yeast mixture and beat again until mixture becomes very gummy. Add lemon extract, vanilla, and butter and beat only until butter is incorporated and dough leaves the sides of bowl. Cover and let rise (if possible over a bowl of warm water) for about 1½ hours.

Grease baba molds lightly. Fill them either by using your hands or with a spoon. They should be not more than half full. Let rise until molds are almost full (but do not let them rise too long—probably about 30 to 45 minutes). Bake at 375° for 25 to 35 minutes (depending on size of molds). Remove from oven and after about 3 or 4 minutes remove babas from molds and cool thoroughly on cake racks.

To make the rum syrup: Using a potato peeler remove peel from orange and lemon and combine with the water and sugar. Quarter orange and lemon and add them too. Bring to a boil and simmer for 4 or 5 minutes. Remove from heat and add the rum.

To soak the babas: Babas should be at room temperature and syrup should be quite warm—or even slightly hot. Dip babas in the syrup, pressing them down to absorb the syrup, then remove and place in a dish. Glaze tops with the strained apricot jam or melted jelly.

To serve: Always serve soaked babas at room temperature. They can be accompanied with any number of different things. You can serve them with:

1. cherries jubilee—
2. whipped cream and strawberries—
3. pastry cream (see recipe on p. 157)—
4. mixture of different fruits of the season—
5. or even softened vanilla ice cream—
6. and see the way they are served in the recipe on p. 189.

To prepare ahead of time: These can be baked one or two days ahead. Place in plastic bag and refrigerate. Before using bring to room temperature, then proceed with dipping them in the warm syrup.

To freeze: These can be baked and frozen. Bring to room temperature, then proceed with the dipping in syrup.

Note: The baba dough can be baked in smaller molds—for example—in tiny cupcake tins, then served as miniature babas. Or they can be baked in small savarin molds, or in one large mold, etc. Adjust baking time according to size of molds.

A PINEAPPLE-PRALINE PARADISE [serves 6]

1 large fresh pineapple	*for the praline ice cream:*
1 orange	1 quart vanilla ice cream
1 cup sugar	⅔ cup sugar
½ cup water	⅔ cup diced almonds

Make the praline ice cream: Place the ⅔ cup of sugar in a heavy skillet and melt over moderate heat, stirring occasionally. As soon as sugar has caramelized add the diced almonds and stir until combined. Be careful not to burn the sugar. Pour this into a lightly greased metal pan and place on a rack until cold. Break this praline in pieces—then—using a wooden mallet or some other heavy object pound it into pea-size pieces. (Cover praline with plastic wrap while you pound it so that it doesn't fly all over your kitchen.)

Place vanilla ice cream in a large bowl. Work in the prepared praline, stirring only as much as is necessary to combine. Refreeze. When frozen scoop into generous size balls. Keep frozen.

Prepare pineapple: Cut pineapple in half lengthwise right through the greenery. Remove pineapple from the shells and dice it. Save the shells for serving.

Remove the orange part of the skin of the orange (but none of the white) and cut it into very fine strips (julienne). Cover orange strips with water and cook for about 5 minutes, then drain and set them aside.

Caramelize the 1 cup of sugar in a heavy skillet over moderate heat, stirring occasionally. Add the ½ cup of water, then cook and stir over low heat until sugar has dissolved. Add orange strips and diced pineapple and cook for 1 minute.

To assemble and serve: Heat pineapple mixture. When warm, strain, saving the sauce. Place pineapple cubes in one of the pineapple shells. Place remaining sauce (to be served hot) in a separate serving dish Place praline ice cream balls in the other empty pineapple shell. Place filled shells on a large serving tray and pass to your guests. Serve the sauce separately.

To prepare ahead of time: Orange-pineapple mixture can be prepared the day before and kept refrigerated. Reheat, then proceed with the recipe.

To freeze: Praline ice cream balls can be done ahead and kept frozen for several days or longer. Keep them well covered.

ONE OF THE SULTAN'S DELIGHTS [serves 6]

Reflections on a triumphal dessert that I ate at Lasserre in Paris.

You will need:

1 ¼ cups *praline powder* (recipe on p. 156)

Caramel lace baskets (recipe follows)

thin slices of sponge or *genoise cake* (recipe on p. 151 or buy some)

kirsch

Praline ice cream (recipe follows)

Poached fresh pears (recipe follows

Crème anglaise with praline (recipe follows)

1 tablespoon soft butter

Caramel lace baskets:

¾ cup butter, melted
½ cup brown sugar
    (pack to measure)
¼ cup sugar

½ cup dark corn syrup
2 teaspoons vanilla
1 ½ cups sifted flour

Combine butter, two kinds of sugar, and corn syrup in a saucepan. Stir over low heat until sugar has dissolved. Remove from heat and beat in the vanilla and flour. Bake wafers two at a time by dropping the prepared batter from a large tablespoon on to a lightly greased cookie sheet. They will spread during the baking so don't attempt more than two at a time. Bake at 300° for about 10 to 12 minutes or until wafers are golden brown.

Remove from oven and let stand briefly—you want them a little firm but not crisp. Remove these large wafers with the aid of a large spatula and drape over the outside of two bowls (dessert size) placed upside down—or around two extra large oranges—molding them into basket shapes. As soon as they are cool place them on sheets of waxed paper or foil and continue with the baking.

This amount makes more baskets than you need, but they keep well and can be used for other desserts. Store them in airtight tins between layers of waxed paper and they will keep several weeks. They can be frozen packed the same way and will keep for months.

Praline ice cream:

1 pint vanilla ice cream

¼ cup of the praline powder listed at the beginning of this recipe

Mix ice cream and praline powder together, then refreeze. Divide into 6 portions after it has become solid, but keep frozen until time to serve.

Poached fresh pears:

6 large fresh pears
3 cups water
1 ¾ cups sugar

several strips of lemon peel
juice of half a lemon
1 teaspoon vanilla

Peel pears leaving them whole and retain the stems. Remove cores through bottom of pears. Combine water, sugar, lemon peel, lemon juice, and vanilla in a large saucepan and bring to a boil, stirring until sugar is dissolved. Simmer for two minutes. Add pears about 3 at a time and poach until tender—about 10 minutes. Do not overcook. Place pears in a large bowl and cover with the syrup. Chill.

Crème anglaise with praline:

2 cups milk, scalded	⅛ teaspoon salt
¼ cup sugar	1 teaspoon vanilla
2 eggs	½ cup praline powder listed
2 egg yolks	at beginning of this recipe

Heat milk. Add sugar and salt and stir to dissolve sugar. Beat eggs and egg yolks in a separate bowl. Add hot mixture to eggs, beating at the same time, then place in the top of a double boiler. Cook, stirring constantly, until custard thickens enough to coat a spoon. Cool rapidly over ice. Add vanilla. Chill, then stir in praline powder. Keep refrigerated until time to serve.

Make a praline stuffing for the pears: Combine the 1 tablespoon of soft butter with the remaining ½ cup of praline powder. Knead together with a spoon to form a paste. Divide into 6 fingers about 1½ inches long. Set aside at room temperature until ready to stuff pears.

To assemble and serve: Drain and dry pears. Stuff each with a finger of praline paste. Place lace baskets on dessert plates. Place a small thin slice of genoise or sponge cake (no more than ¼ inch thick) on the inside of the basket and brush each with a little kirsch. Place a portion of the praline ice cream on top of each. Flatten gently. Place stuffed pears on top of the ice cream. Pass the crème anglaise with praline— or—spoon it on generously before passing plates to guests.

Note: Be sure that guests are provided with both dessert forks and spoons.

To prepare ahead of time: The praline powder (see recipe on p. 156) and the caramel lace baskets can be made at least one week ahead. The cake, the crème anglaise with praline, and the poached pears can be made the day before. (The ice cream should be prepared ahead and frozen; see below.)

To freeze: The praline ice cream must be done ahead and frozen. The praline powder, the caramel lace baskets, and the cake can all be frozen.

A TRIPLE RASPBERRY TREAT [serves about 16]

An interpretation—not a replica—of the unique raspberry dessert served at Chez Garin in Paris.

one 4-egg *sponge roll* (recipe on p. 166) without jelly; do not roll, just turn out, remove waxed paper, and leave flat.

3 quarts raspberry ice or sherbert

4 packages frozen raspberries, defrosted

4 or 5 boxes fresh raspberries

1½ cups heavy cream, whipped, then sweetened and flavored with framboise or kirsch liqueur

Cut sponge roll in three equal parts—crosswise, not lengthwise. Using the three parts as layers for a cake, assemble in this way: Place one layer on a flat board (bread board of some kind is particularly good for this). Cover with 1½ quarts of the raspberry ice or sherbet. Place second cake layer on top, then cover with remaining ice or sherbet. Top with third layer and press down. Smooth sides with a knife or spatula. Cover this whole thing with plastic wrap and foil and freeze.

Whirl defrosted raspberries (one package at a time) in a blender, then strain through a sieve to remove the seeds. Refrigerate this purée in a decorative bowl covered with plastic wrap. Arrange whipped, sweetened, and flavored cream in a bowl and chill. Arrange fresh raspberries in an attractive dish BUT DO NOT REFRIGERATE. Berries are far more delicious served at room temperature.

To serve: This can all be done at table. Bring frozen cake, purée, whipped cream, and raspberries to dining table or side table. Use plates of ample size—dinner plate size is best. Place a thin slice of the frozen raspberry ice cake on each guest's plate. Place a small bouquet of fresh raspberries on either side of the cake slice. Spoon a little of the purée on the fresh raspberries (but not on the cake). Then, pass the whipped cream so that guests help themselves. It is important to keep the cake slice separate from the berries and purée to achieve a beautiful uncluttered, unstacked effect; this is the reason for large plates.

To prepare ahead of time: The cake can be baked the day before.

To freeze: The cake filled with raspberry ice or sherbet can be wrapped and kept frozen for about 2 weeks.

CHOCOLATE CUPS WITH COFFEE ICE CREAM AND FILBERTS [serves about 8]

In the manner of the Hostellerie du Prieuré near Chenùtte les Tuffeaux.

8 *Chocolate cups*
  (recipe below)
1 quart coffee ice cream
  (or a little less)
48 toasted filberts

for decoration:
  tiny strips of angelica
  chopped pistachios or
  chopped filberts

Chocolate cups:
½ pound dark sweet
  chocolate
3 tablespoons butter

paper baking cups and
  muffin pans

Melt chocolate and butter together over warm water. Remove from heat and stir until blended. Cool for a few minutes.

Place paper baking cups inside muffin pans (the regular size). Using a teaspoon swirl chocolate around the sides and bottoms of the paper cups, covering them completely with a thin layer of chocolate. Chill. Check to see if all the paper has been covered; if not, repair any thin spots or tiny holes with dabs (thin) of the melted chocolate. Chill again. Later peel off the paper cups and return chocolate cups to refrigerator until time to use.

To assemble: Fill each chocolate cup with a small scoop of coffee ice cream—mounding it high like an ice cream cone. Place six toasted filberts around the edge of the chocolate cups. Sprinkle top with chopped nuts and decorate the center tops with angelica strips.

To prepare ahead of time: Chocolate cups can be made several days before. Keep covered and refrigerated.

To freeze: The chocolate cups can be filled with the ice cream, covered with plastic wrap, and frozen two or three days before serving. (Be sure they are well covered if you plan to freeze them a few days ahead. If they are to remain in the freezer for just a few hours no wrapping is necessary.) Add filberts, angelica and chopped nuts shortly before serving.

Hint: Serve these with both dessert forks and spoons.

1 large sponge cake with
   a hole in the center
   (buy or bake)
½ quart vanilla ice cream
½ quart strawberry
   sherbert (or
   boysenberry)

for rum syrup:
½ cup sugar
½ cup water
½ cup dark Jamaican
   rum
1 cup whipping cream
1 tablespoon sugar
1 teaspoon vanilla

Make rum syrup: Boil sugar and water together, stirring until sugar has dissolved. Remove from heat and stir in rum.

To assemble: Cut cake in three horizontal layers. Place one layer on a serving dish and douse with rum syrup. Cover this evenly with the vanilla ice cream. Next a second layer of cake doused with syrup, then topped with the strawberry sherbet. Top with the third cake layer and soak this too with the syrup. Place in freezer to harden while you whip the cream with the 1 tablespoon of sugar and the vanilla.

Decorate the frozen gâteau with dabs and swirls of whipped cream. If you can handle a pastry bag use it and make decorative rosettes, etc. Return to freezer and as soon as whipped cream has frozen cover with plastic wrap or aluminum foil. Remove from freezer ½ hour before serving.

Note: This can be served as is—or—it can be accompanied with a chocolate sauce or some kind of strawberry or other fruit sauce.

To prepare ahead of time: If you are making the sponge cake it can be baked a day ahead.

To freeze: The assembled gâteau (well wrapped) will keep nicely in the freezer for several weeks.

COFFEE RUM RAISIN MOUSSE [serves about 10]

Partly based on some recollections of a beautiful coffee dessert served at Le Petit Auberge de Noves near Avignon.

3 egg yolks
½ cup sugar
⅛ teaspoon salt
¾ cup strong coffee
   (use boiling water
   plus 4 teaspoons
   instant coffee)
1½ teaspoons gelatin soaked
   in 3 tablespoons
   of cold water

½ cup raisins
¼ cup dark Jamaican
   rum
1½ cups whipping
   cream
¼ cup praline powder
   (optional), but see
   recipe on p. 156

Soak raisins in rum for several hours (or overnight). Soak the gelatin. Combine egg yolks, sugar, and salt in the top of a double boiler. Beat in the coffee. Cook over simmering water, stirring, until a thin custard is achieved. Stir in soaked gelatin. Add raisins and rum and cool over ice, stirring, until cool but not firm. Stir in praline powder. Whip cream until stiff, then fold in custard. Freeze either in small molds or in demitasse cups.

To serve: If frozen in molds, unmold and place on dessert plates; if in demitasse cups serve directly from the cups.

Note: If dessert is unmolded it can be served with a very thin cold chocolate sauce or with a dab of whipped cream. If dessert is served in cups it can be topped with a dab of whipped cream plus a tiny tiny sprinkling of praline powder or powdered coffee or finely chopped nuts.

CAFÉ LIÉGEOIS [serves 6]

My interpretation of a French classic.

1 quart coffee ice cream
powdered instant coffee
1 cup whipping cream

2 tablespoons sugar
2 tablespoons cognac

If possible use large stemmed goblets for this. Place a small scoop of ice cream in each glass. Sprinkle each with ¼ teaspoon of powdered coffee. Repeat with ice cream and powdered coffee. Place in freezer while preparing the cream.

Whip cream, then sweeten with the sugar and flavor with cognac. Spoon this mixture on top of the ice cream in the glasses. Top each with a few grains of the powdered coffee.

To freeze: These can be assembled as much as a week ahead and kept frozen but each glass must be covered tightly with plastic wrap. If frozen ahead of time, remove from freezer about 20 to 30 minutes before serving.

PÊCHE MELBA [serves 8]

1 quart of vanilla ice cream	*for the Melba sauce:*
4 fresh ripe peaches	1 10-ounce package frozen raspberries
½ cup sliced almonds, toasted	1 10-ounce jar currant jelly

Make the sauce: Defrost raspberries, whirl in a blender, then put through a sieve to remove seeds. Combine with the currant jelly and heat and stir until jelly has melted. Remove from heat and cool, then chill.

Peel peaches and cut in half. Top servings of vanilla ice cream with the peach halves, spoon on some Melba sauce and sprinkle with the toasted sliced almonds.

To prepare ahead of time: Peaches can be peeled in the morning and kept in lemon juice and water in the refrigerator. Drain and dry them before using. Melba sauce can be made in the morning.

To freeze: If you have room in your freezer it is a good idea to arrange the ice cream in the serving bowls and keep them in the freezer until time to serve.

PÊCHE MADELEINE [serves 4]

A variation on "pêche Melba" but fewer calories; I ate something like this one summer at Lucas Carton in Paris.

4 peeled fresh peaches
24 blanched almonds, toasted

1 carton frozen raspberries
fresh raspberries

Purée raspberries (having defrosted them). Put through a sieve to remove seeds.

Place whole peaches on individual plates and stick 6 almonds in each. Spoon raspberry purée over peaches and surround with a few raspberries.

To prepare ahead of time: Peaches can be peeled in the morning. Keep them refrigerated in a bowl of lemon juice and water. Drain and dry thoroughly before using. Purée can be prepared in the morning too; keep refrigerated until time to serve.

AN AMSTERDAM COFFEE DESSERT [serves 8]

1 quart of vanilla ice cream

for walnut praline:
  1 cup sugar
  1 cup coarsely chopped walnuts

for the coffee syrup:
  1 cup water
  1 heaping tablespoon powdered coffee
  ¼ cup sugar
  1 teaspoon cornstarch
  ¼ cup cold water

Make the praline: Melt the 1 cup of sugar in a heavy skillet over moderate heat, stirring until it caramelizes. Add walnuts and as soon as they are well combined with the caramel pour into a greased metal pan. Cool completely, then chop or grind coarsely (do not put in a blender). Place in a tightly sealed glass jar and keep refrigerated.

Make the coffee syrup: Boil the 1 cup of water, then add coffee and sugar. Simmer gently for about 5 minutes. Dissolve cornstarch in the ¼ cup of cold water and add. Stir constantly until mixture simmers again. Cool, then chill.

To serve: Place portions of vanilla ice cream in dessert bowls. Spoon on some of the chilled coffee syrup, then top with some of the chopped walnut praline.

To prepare ahead of time: Both the praline and the coffee syrup can be made a week or so ahead; keep refrigerated.

PAPAYAS FILLED WITH FRUIT—SERVED WITH BANANA CREAM   [serves 6]

3 large ripe papayas
½ honeydew melon
2 or 3 plums, peeled
   and sliced
2 cups diced fresh
   pineapple
fresh raspberries or
   strawberries

for the banana cream:
2 ripe bananas
juice of half a lime
¼ cup coconut syrup
   (or honey)
⅔ cup whipping cream

Cut papayas in half and remove seeds. Scoop out flesh using a small melon ball scooper. Reserve the shells. Scoop honeydew melon into small balls. Combine papaya, pineapple, honeydew, and sliced plums. (If you want to add sugar do so to your taste.) Cover and refrigerate.

Make the banana cream: Mash the bananas with the lime juice. Mix in the coconut syrup. Whip cream, then fold in banana mixture. Refrigerate (covered) briefly.

To serve: Fill papaya shells with the mixed fruit and top each serving with a few raspberries or strawberries. Serve at table and pass the banana cream. (Or you can spoon the banana cream over each filled papaya and then top with the raspberries or strawberries.)

To prepare ahead of time: Fruit can be prepared and refrigerated in the morning. The banana cream should not be mixed more than 3 or 4 hours ahead.

SHADES OF PINK DESSERT [serves 6]

1 pint of raspberry ice
or sherbet
36 fresh bing cherries,
pitted

48 watermelon balls
sugar to taste
¼ cup framboise liqueur
6 tiny fresh mint sprigs

Using a melon ball scooper scoop raspberry ice into very small balls. Keep frozen until time to serve.

Combine pitted cherries and watermelon balls. Sweeten to taste and add the framboise. Cover and chill.

To serve: Divide the raspberry ice or sherbet balls among six individual dessert bowls. Top each with some of the bing cherries and watermelon balls. Decorate with mint sprigs and serve at once.

To prepare ahead of time: Watermelon balls and cherries can be prepared in the morning; keep covered and refrigerated.

To freeze: The raspberry ice or sherbet balls can be put directly into the dessert bowls and placed in the freezer in the morning. Just before serving add the fruit.

STRAWBERRIES ROMANOFF-MELLINKOFF
[serves about 12]

1 ½ quarts of vanilla ice
cream
5 baskets of fresh
strawberries

½ cup Grand Marnier
sugar to taste
2 or 3 cups whipping cream

Place strawberries in a very large bowl. They should only half fill the bowl and it should be one that you can serve from. If you don't have one large enough then divide them in two. Sweeten to taste and add Grand Marnier.

Scoop ice cream into a bowl and return to freezer until 1 hour before serving. Ice cream needs to be slightly soft but not melted.

Whip cream and place in a bowl.

To serve: Bring all bowls to table along with individual dessert bowls. Before your guests do the following:

1. Stir softened ice cream into the marinated strawberries, but do not overmix.
2. Fold whipped cream into the strawberry-ice cream mixture.
3. Now, spoon this into the individual dessert bowls and serve to each guest.

Note: I prefer the strawberries marinated at room temperature. Keep the bowl (or bowls) tightly covered with plastic wrap; stir occasionally during the day.

To prepare ahead of time: Strawberries can be prepared in the morning. Cream can be whipped and refrigerated several hours ahead.

PAT ALTMAN'S TERRIFIC TORREJAS
[Serves about 8, 3 pancakes per guest]

For the syrup:
2 cups dark brown sugar
(pack to measure)
4 cups water
3 sticks cinnamon

For the pancakes:
6 eggs (warmed slightly in
a bowl of hot water)

½ cup fine bread crumbs
(commercial kind okay)
butter for frying

For the garnish:
whipped cream
sugar
vanilla

Prepare the syrup. Combine ingredients in a large skillet and cook uncovered over moderate heat until slightly thickened, then reduce heat so syrup just simmers. Meanwhile make the pancakes.

Beat eggs with an electric mixer until very thick (almost like whipped cream). Fold in bread crumbs.

Heat a very heavy skillet or griddle and butter lightly. Using a ¼ cup measuring cup (or ladle holding that amount) fry the pancakes, turning once or twice until brown.

Pancakes will not spread much and at first will be quite thick. As each group of pancakes is done add them to the syrup, basting with the syrup. Remove pancakes to a large platter after they are well soaked (thus making room for others to be immersed in the syrup). When finished most of the syrup will have been absorbed by the pancakes. Dribble whatever is left over the pancakes on the platter. Cover with plastic wrap and serve at room temperature. Garnish with whipped cream that has been lightly sweetened and flavored with vanilla.

To prepare ahead of time: These can be made a day ahead. Cover and refrigerate but bring them to room temperature before serving.

To freeze: These can be frozen—wrap pancakes in foil. To serve, defrost, then reheat in a moderate oven, then place on platter and bring to room temperature before serving.

Note: I like these served hot too—and they reheat beautifully in the oven.

PEACHES CARAMELLED AND FLAMBÉED [serves 4]

Vaguely inspired by a dessert we were served at the Hotel de la Poste in Beaune.

2 fresh peaches, peeled and halved	1 ounce kirsch
4 tablespoons sugar	1 ounce Grand Marnier
2 tablespoons butter	½ ounce 151 proof rum
¼ cup sliced almonds, toasted	4 large scoops vanilla ice cream

Put ice cream in large individual dessert bowls and place in freezer. Leave them there until the last possible moment.

Bring chafing dish and the rest of the ingredients to table; this should be prepared before your guests.

Place sugar in chafing dish and stir slowly until it melts and begins to caramelize. Add butter and peaches and stir gently, turning the peaches occasionally until sugar, butter, and juices combine. Sprinkle with the almonds, then add the kirsch and Grand Marnier and stir. Add the 151 proof rum, flame at once and serve half a peach, some of the almonds, and some of the sauce on each serving of ice cream.

Hint: Don't bring the ice cream to table until almost time to flambé the peaches. The dessert is at its best if the ice cream is very hard when the hot peaches and sauce are added.

To prepare ahead of time: Arrange all the ingredients except ice cream on a tray and place on a side board. This can be done in the morning. If peaches are peeled ahead of time, rub them with a little lemon juice and make certain that they are tightly covered with plastic wrap.

BLUEBERRY AND PEACH CRISP [serves about 6]

2 cups fresh blueberries
6 fresh peaches, peeled
   and sliced

for the topping:
¾ cup flour

pinch of salt
1 cup brown sugar
   (pack to measure)
3 tablespoons soft butter
½ teaspoon cinnamon

Combine the ingredients for the topping—use your fingers or a pastry blender.

Place fruit in a casserole or quiche dish. Sprinkle with the topping and bake at 350° for about 45 minutes.

Serve hot or cold. If desired, ice cream or whipped cream can be served with this.

To prepare ahead of time: This can be baked in the morning.

To freeze: This can be frozen. Do not overbake. Defrost, then reheat before serving.

SLOANE SQUARE APPLES [serves 3 to 4]

As I did them in London one early spring.

½ to ⅔ cup sugar
3 cups sliced apples
   (use green ones)
2 small oranges

2 tablespoons butter
1 tablespoon Grand Marnier
   or other orange liqueur
heavy cream

Remove orange part of orange peel with a potato peeler or a sharp knife. Cut it in tiny strips (julienne). Squeeze oranges for juice.

Melt sugar in a heavy skillet and as soon as it has caramelized add the sliced apples, stir, and add orange juice, peel, and butter and Grand Marnier. Cook over moderate heat, stirring, just until apples are tender.

Serve warm and pass the heavy cream (unwhipped).

To prepare ahead of time: This can be cooked in the morning. Reduce cooking time, then reheat before serving.

To freeze: This can be cooked and frozen. Reduce cooking time. Defrost, then reheat before serving.

BANANA FRITTERS [serves about 8]

for the batter:

2 eggs	4 to 6 bananas, cut in
½ teaspoon salt	thirds
1 cup sifted flour	powdered sugar
1 teaspoon baking powder	sweetened and flavored
2 teaspoons sugar	whipped cream
2 teaspoons lemon juice	(with vanilla)
1 tablespoon oil	
½ to ⅔ cup milk	

Prepare batter: Beat eggs. Sift dry ingredients together and add alternately with the milk. Add the oil and lemon juice. Let stand about an hour if possible. Batter should be the thickness of a pancake batter —or perhaps a little heavier.

To prepare fritters: Before serving dip banana chunks in the batter, then deep fat fry (at about 375°) for approximately 2 minutes. Drain on paper towels, sprinkle with powdered sugar and serve hot with the prepared whipped cream.

To prepare ahead of time: Batter can be prepared several hours ahead of time. Keep refrigerated until almost time to fry the fritters.

SIENESE PANFORTE

An ancient and noble confection from Siena—presented here *à ma façon*.

4 ounces candied orange peel (about ¾ cup finely chopped)
4 ounces candied lemon peel (about ¾ cup finely chopped)
4 ounces candied citron (about ¾ cup finely chopped)
4 ounces diced or shredded (but not sliced) almonds, toasted (about 1 cup)
4 ounces filberts, toasted and skins removed, then coarsely chopped (about 1 cup)

⅔ cup sifted flour
¼ cup unsweetened cocoa
1 ½ teaspoons cinnamon
¼ teaspoon allspice
⅔ cup honey
⅔ cup sugar
1 teaspoon vanilla

for later:

2 tablespoons powdered sugar sifted together with 1 tablespoon cinnamon

Place chopped orange and lemon peel, citron, almonds, and filberts in a large bowl. Combine flour, cocoa, cinnamon, and allspice in a smaller bowl and mix thoroughly, then pour over the fruit-nut mixture and mix. Use your hands for this job—you want each piece of fruit and each nut well coated.

Combine sugar and honey in a saucepan and stir over low heat until mixture comes to a boil. Cook slowly over moderate heat, stirring occasionally, until a little forms a soft ball in cold water. Remove from heat and add vanilla. Pour over the coated fruit-nut mixture and stir until thoroughly combined.

Grease two 7- or 8-inch spring form pans. Line bottom of each pan with a circle of waxed paper. Grease paper. Line sides of pans with strips of waxed paper and grease insides of those too. Spoon stiff mixture into these prepared pans, pressing down and smoothing tops with a spoon or with your hands. Bake at 300° for approximately 45 minutes.

Remove from oven and place on racks to cool until solid enough to turn out (about 15 to 20 minutes). Turn upside down on well greased foil, then carefully remove waxed paper. When cakes are completely cold, sprinkle tops and bottoms with the sifted powdered sugar-cinnamon mixture. Wrap cakes in waxed paper then in foil. Store on your pantry shelf. Cut in small wedges to serve.

To prepare ahead of time: This really must be made ahead of time—at least one week, several are better. The panforte will keep many many months if kept tightly wrapped in heavy layers of foil.

Index